The Canning Diva®

—— PRESENTS ——

MEALS IN A JAR

DIANE DEVEREAUX

TEN PEAKS PRESS®
EUGENE, OR

Published in association with Tom Dean, literary agent with A Drop of Ink LLC, www.adropofink.pub

Cover design by Faceout Studio, Amanda Hudson
Interior design by Faceout Studio, Paul Nielsen
Photography by Jeff Hage/Green Frog Photo

Neither the author nor publisher is responsible for any outcome from use of this cookbook. The recipes are intended for informational purposes and those who have the appropriate culinary skills. USDA guidelines should always be followed in food preparation and canning. The author and publisher make no warranty, express or implied, in any recipe.

For bulk or special sales, please call 1-800-547-8979. Email: CustomerService@hhpbooks.com

 TEN PEAKS PRESS is a federally registered trademark of The Hawkins Children's LLC. Harvest House Publishers, Inc., is the exclusive licensee of this trademark.
THE CANNING DIVA is a registered trademark of Devereaux Cyber Inc. Specific, limited use of THE CANNING DIVA trademark has been granted to Harvest House Publishers, Inc.

THE CANNING DIVA® PRESENTS MEALS IN A JAR

Copyright © 2024 by Diane Devereaux, The Canning Diva˙
Foreword copyright © 2024 by Carrie Underwood
Published by Ten Peaks Press, an imprint of Harvest House Publishers
Eugene, Oregon 97408

ISBN 978-0-7369-8911-4 (pbk.)
ISBN 978-0-7369-8912-1 (eBook)

Library of Congress Control Number: 2024931099

Printed in the United States of America

24 25 26 27 28 29 30 31 32/ VP—FO /10 9 8 7 6 5 4 3 2 1

To my first and forever best
friend, my beautiful sister, Deborah.
Your compassion and tenacity are an
inspiration to me and countless others.
Thank you for always being there for
me and for believing in me when
I doubted myself.

Contents

Foreword

by Carrie Underwood

I'm a farm girl. Always have been. Always will be. I was born in Oklahoma in the 1980s before the rise of the internet, before social media, before everything was "on demand," and before the days of everyone being so impossibly busy. As a child, I remember taking Sunday drives to my grandmother's house where we would just sit and visit with each other. I would play outside, and she would whip up delicious meals. Stews and roasts and cobblers that were nothing fancy by any means, but they sure were yummy! She was part of a generation that ate what they had available to them, and they stretched every ingredient as far as it would go. There was nothing wasted, and they relied on ways of preserving food that have been lost on the generations since. I have always longed to learn those ways but had no idea where to start.

I have been beyond blessed to have an amazing career that has taken me to places that I never could have dreamed, but, in the midst of it all, I found myself lacking roots. All the bright lights and hotels and travel left me feeling disconnected from nature and so many of the things that could truly satisfy my soul. So, I did what any farm girl would do. I started a garden, bought some chickens, learned how to make bread, and began figuring out how to do things that probably would've come so naturally to my grandmother. I bought a pressure canner and began reading and looking up recipes, and I realized that pressure canning seemed very complicated. To be honest, that canner sat in its box in a closet downstairs for quite some time. Pressure canning actually scared me! I truly thought that if I made even one small error,

6

I would blow up my entire kitchen! In my internet searches trying to find someone—anyone— who could make it all make sense, I stumbled across Diane Devereaux, a.k.a. "The Canning Diva." All her recipes sounded so yummy and practical. I rarely saw any recipe that had things I didn't already have in my kitchen. She made it seem like even I could figure out the art of pressure canning. And, to be honest, I liked her vibe. I reached out to Diane and actually got to meet her and have a fun girls' day where some friends and I learned the basics of canning. Since that day, I am a changed woman! I can all the time now. I make use of my garden goodness and of the things that my husband hunts…using Diane's books as my guides, of course. It's so nice to know that, in the midst of all the craziness that life brings—from my kids' basketball practices, baseball games, taekwondo lessons, skating lessons, and all the school functions, to my own rehearsals, shows and all the things that my job has me running to—I always have some delicious and nutritious ready-made meals that I can quickly heat up that help keep us all gathered around the dinner table in the evenings for that oh-so-important family time. Plus, canning is super fun!

So, whether you're an expert canner or this is your first go at it, trust me when I tell you that you're in good hands with the Diva! May we all enjoy this process together and do our part to make sure this art and these skills are passed on to a new generation! Happy canning!

The Principles of Pressure Canning

In this chapter you will learn the many benefits of preserving low-acid foods and the science and math used to help us home canners preserve food for long-term storage. I will take you through the history of home canning, educating you on the principles discovered and still used to this day. This chapter will also give you the basis for preserving food in jars and how processing and cooling plays a vital role in our safety. Further, you will gain knowledge of various foodborne pathogens and microorganisms and how to avoid them when home canning. Last, I will teach you the significance of proper storage techniques so you may lengthen the life span of your home-canned goods.

THE HISTORY OF PRESSURE CANNING

While the birth of home canning can be attributed to the Napoleonic Wars, home canning truly started in 1792 amid the French Revolution. Napoleon was losing the war because by the time the food made it from his kingdom to the front line, it was rotted and inedible. As the saying goes, "An army marches on its stomach." Thus, in 1795, a campaign was launched with a 12,000-franc reward to the person who could invent a method for preserving large quantities of food long term. Nicolas Appert worked for many years to solve this problem, finally claiming the award in 1810. Rather than squandering his winnings, Appert chose to invest the money into developing the first commercial cannery, the House of Appert, which operated from 1812 to 1933.

Well over a hundred years prior, however, the first pressure cooker was invented. It was invented in 1679 to be exact, by Denis Papin, a French-born British physicist, mathematician, and inventor. He was born in 1647 and originally wanted to be a doctor. Papin achieved his goal and received his MD in 1669. However, his true passion was for math and mechanics. So Papin left the world of medicine and became a skillful mechanic who aided in the construction of a vacuum pump. He published his research in 1674, describing the various tests he performed, including attempts to preserve food within a vacuum. From this work he later invented the pressure cooker, which back then was called a steam digester.

The steam digester was a closed vessel with a tight-fitting lid that confined the steam until a high pressure was generated, which considerably raised the boiling point—or temperature—of the water within the vessel. Papin is also known for inventing a safety valve to prevent explosions, given the amount of pressure the closed vessel would create. This steam digester was used to extract meat from, and soften, animal bones, which were later dried to create bonemeal.

Fast forward to the mid-1800s, when a man named Louis Pasteur was making his mark in history. Pasteur discovered how bacteria was responsible for the souring of wine. This led him to be able to prove why food spoiled, due to microorganisms and foodborne pathogens. This discovery led to his development of a process called *pasteurization*. Pasteurization uses high temperatures between 140°F (60°C) and 212°F (100°C) to heat foods, then letting them cool, which kills harmful microorganisms in high-acid foods. The higher the temperature, the shorter the time exposed. This process is still used to this day in the food industry and home canning.

It was Pasteur who understood how time, temperature, and acidic value play a vital role in preserving food and Papin and Appert who designed the mechanisms to do so. The temperature and time of pasteurization treatments (processing) are determined by the recipe's overall acidity and density.

With discoveries in mechanics, food spoilage, and processing now known, pressure canner manufacturers began to emerge in the marketplace. In 1864 Georg Gutbrod of Stuttgart, Germany, started manufacturing pressure cookers made of tinned cast iron. In 1890 Archibald Kenrick & Sons in England manufactured a 6-quart pressure cooker. At the start of the 1900s, commercial pressure canning made its way to America. In 1905, Northwestern Steel and Iron Works in Wisconsin manufactured commercial "canner retorts," large-scale pressure canners, for the food industry and hotels. They later changed their name to National Pressure Cooker Company and focused their efforts on the consumer market, becoming one of the largest companies in America to make pressure canners to preserve low-acid foods in the home.

By 1915 the in-home use of pressure canners was born. And in 1917 the US Department of Agriculture (USDA) recommended to consumers all low-acid foods should be processed by use of a pressure canner rather than water bathing. This recommendation further catapulted the manufacture and sale of in-home, consumer-use pressure canners. However, as more people began to consume commercially canned foods, a rise in foodborne illnesses occurred.

Improper processing methods and controls within the commercial canning industry resulted in the survival of microorganisms within the canned food, making people very sick when consumed. From 1918 to 1921, much attention was

focused on botulism in commercially canned products. Because the home-canning processing times were loosely derived from the commercial-canning industry, preserving low-acid foods in the home had its own outbreaks of botulism poisoning. Roughly twelve people per year were sickened with botulism poisoning from improper home-canning techniques.

Benefits of Using a Digital Pressure Canner

While there are many reasons to pressure-can food for long-term storage, here are a few reasons to invest in a digital pressure canner:

1. Provides precise temperature control, which avoids the vast temperature swings that are common with stovetop canners and helps maintain the food's integrity and avoid overprocessing.

2. Greatly reduces liquid siphoning from jars during processing, dramatically reducing lid-sealing failures.

3. Gives home canners freedom to attend to other matters in the home without having to constantly monitor the stovetop.

4. Makes pressure canning much more convenient, providing an easy option for preserving leftovers or food snatched up during unplanned grocery store deals. My digital canner rarely leaves my countertop as I have incorporated canning into my everyday life.

While efforts succeeded in remedying outbreaks in the commercial food-canning industry, it wasn't until 1945 that researchers invested sufficient time and money into testing processes for home canning. Three valid discoveries during this testing helped improve the food quality and safety of home canning low-acid meats and vegetables.

First, using a glass jar when home canning produces a slower heating and exhausting time, which is much different from preserving in commercial tin or aluminum cans. Second, home-canned foods take much longer to cool after the glass jars are removed from the pressure canner. This increases the sterilization effect, a very positive occurrence, which contributes significantly to killing harmful pathogens because the food is still heating during cooling. Yes, you read that correctly. After removing the jars from the pressure canner to cool and seal, cooler spots within the jar get heated, extending the processing and safety of the food in jars.

And third, home canners had been overprocessing foods out of fear, using such high temperatures that vegetables were rendered extremely mushy and ill tasting. The research concluded and recommended a reduction in processing time and temperature to protect the quality of the food while keeping it safe for human consumption.

The totality of this research was published as *Home Canning Processes for Low-Acid Foods: Developed on the Basis of Heat Penetration and Inoculated Packs*. These standards were adopted by the US Department of Agriculture on December 5, 1946. This research became the foundation of home canning recommendations and guidelines. It is the same foundation that has since informed the design and manufacture of home canning appliances.

In the 1980s, thanks to grant money, cooperative efforts between university extension services and the USDA led to the development of updated home-canning resources. These partnerships have continued in recent years, but due to the lack of federal funding, many canning-recipe creators hire independent laboratories to test new recipes using the same heat penetration and thermal-processing guidelines discovered in 1946.

While research on home canning has stalled at the federal level, advancements in technology have soared. The first electric digital canner hit the market in the early 2000s, and although it was simply an electric water bather with a small capacity, it aided families with electric stovetops and smaller kitchens. It processed 3 quart-size jars or 4 pint-size jars at a time. Roughly twenty years later, National Presto Industries stirred tons of excitement when they created a large-capacity electric canner with digital controls designed to safely process both high- and low-acid foods using the 1946 USDA guidelines. This larger vessel permits canners to pressure-can up to 5 quarts, or 8 pints, or 10 half pints at a time.

PRESSURE CANNING 101

There are two methods of thermal processing: water bathing and pressure canning. Water bathing is typically reserved for high-acid foods like fruit and salsa while pressure canning is used to preserve low-acid foods like meats, vegetables, and meals in a jar. The beauty of home canning as a way of food preservation is there will always be synergy between the two methods of processing, often the ability to interchange the two. For instance, most stovetop pressure canners can double as a water bather, and you may process many high-acid foods using a pressure canner by simply lowering the temperature (PSI) and processing time.

How Water Bathing Works

Foods with an acidic value between 1.0 and 4.6 pH can be safely preserved in a jar by processing the jars under water with a water temperature of 212°F (100°C) for a specified period of time. This method is ample to kill harmful microorganisms and bacteria, which cause foodborne illnesses. Because of the presence of acid, we may use boiling water temperature, pasteurization, and a shorter processing time to adequately denature anything harmful for human consumption.

This processing method is accomplished by fully submerging the glass jars filled with food in water and using very high heat to bring the canner to a full rolling boil on the stovetop. We are relying on the temperature of the water to process the food inside the jars, so if any of the jar is exposed to air and not submerged, bacteria will grow in the exposed food and rot its contents during storage.

Can You Pressure-Can Fruit?

Pressure canning fruit takes less time than water bath canning and gains higher yields. Now, some may argue it takes longer to use a pressure canner and the high heat will render the fruit mushy and inedible. This belief is based on a misconception that a pressure canner must process everything using the same PSI (pounds per square inch) of pressure, regardless of acidity. But that couldn't be further from the truth. Thankfully, pressure canners offer a range of temperature settings, and high-acid foods like fruit can be safely preserved in less time and at a lower temperature.

At 5 PSI we are increasing the temperature slightly past the boiling point to 227°F (108°C). This gentle increase allows us to decrease the processing time compared to the processing time required when using a water bath. And, when using a tall pressure canner, you may stack your jars using a second (or third) flat rack, dramatically increasing your yield. The alternative would be multiple batches in a water bather versus everything loaded into one pressure canner.

How Pressure Canning Works

Foods with an acidic value between 4.7 and 9.0 pH can be safely preserved in a jar by processing the jars in a vessel designed to create pressure with an air temperature of 240°F (116°C) or higher for a specified period of time. This method of processing foods is ample to not only kill harmful microorganisms and bacteria but also keep the food's integrity intact. Because of the lack of acid, this method of processing relies solely on very high temperature and time to denature anything harmful for consumption.

The only way this process can be accomplished is by using an airtight vessel such as a pressure canner. Pressure canning relies on air pressure to create a temperature above the boiling point. Further, we must achieve a temperature of 240°F (116°C) so the heat both fully penetrates the food and denatures harmful foodborne pathogens.

Outside of temperature differences, pressure canning differs from water bathing by the way in which we fill the vessel. When using a pressure canner, the jars are no longer submerged in water but rather sit on a flat rack with a limited amount of water inside the vessel. For first-time canners who have only water bathed, it can be very unnerving to see your jars not covered in water. Not to worry! Embrace the difference and feel secure knowing your foods in jars are exactly as they need to be when pressure canning.

The pressurized air within the canner accomplishes the thermal processing. The water placed in the pressure canner prevents a "dry can." In other words, it prevents the canner from operating dry, which, under such extreme heat conditions, could warp or bow the bottom of the canner, likely destroying it and preventing any future use. It could also overheat the glass jars, causing them to break. If your canner and jars are not destroyed when the canner runs dry, you will notice the food in each jar is burnt in appearance and in flavor. It is imperative you follow your pressure canner manual to ensure you give your canner the proper amount of water prior to filling it with jars to process.

THE THREE PILLARS OF HOME CANNING

As you read through the history of home canning, it is easy to see the progression of knowledge and understanding of how time, temperature, and acidic value play such a vital role in keeping our food safe for long-term storage and consumption. Let's take a minute to dive into the science and math behind home canning to learn more about what I call the "Three Pillars": acidic pH value, time, and temperature.

Acidic pH Value. In home canning, it is the recipe's overall acidic pH value that dictates how much time and at what temperature the recipe must be exposed to heat (processing) to kill harmful microorganisms and pathogens. For instance, in this book each recipe will have a lower acidic value (6.5 to 9.0 pH). This means we are without enough acid to deter the growth of bacteria, so we must rely on a higher temperature (240°F [116°C] or higher) for a greater length of time (75 to 160 minutes) to create a safe environment for shelf stability.

As you can see in the chart, every food has its own pH value. I still find it fascinating how a

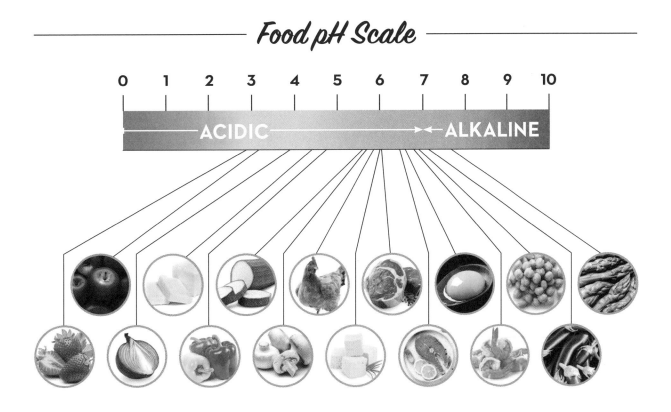

Food pH Scale

beautiful little strawberry has more acid than an intense habanero pepper. Acidity in home canning isn't about "acidic flavor" or something tasting "spicy." It is about the food's chemical makeup. As indicated on the chart, the majority of vegetables and meat are less acidic than fruit, whereas legumes and fish have little to no acid. The food's pH may also change when exposed to heat, meaning some foods will become less or more acidic when cooked.

Time and Temperature. The last two pillars have a unique relationship and are reliant on the recipe's overall pH value and the recipe's density, or thickness. Once the acidity and density of the recipe is understood, we then know which method of processing (water bathing or pressure canning) to use and at what length of time to process. Because of the studies conducted to learn how long a food type must process before harmful microorganisms and pathogens are denatured, we know how these two important pillars play a vital role in preserving our food.

As you can see in the temperature chart, without the presence of acid, we must rely on a higher temperature for a longer period of time to denature harmful pathogens. In contrast, if the recipe has a higher acidic content, we may then process for a shorter period of time using a lower temperature.

Let's break down a salsa recipe together. A typical canning recipe for salsa has a higher ratio of tomatoes, which are acidic. However, the same canning recipe may also include less-acidic ingredients like corn, black beans, onions, and jalapeños. The ratio of acidic ingredients

is presumably higher, yet the combined ratio of lower-acid ingredients decreases the recipe's overall, or total, pH value. The totality of the recipe's ingredients provides the overall pH value used to determine its required exposure time to heat.

In the event we wish to heighten the overall acidic value, we do so by adding acid. This additional acid could be in the form of more tomatoes, or by the addition of vinegar or lime juice. The reason we'd wish to heighten the acid isn't because the recipe is somehow unsafe when lower in acid but rather because heightening the acid decreases the processing time and thus protects the integrity of the food. Overprocessing renders the salsa inedible by producing an overly mushy texture. This is a waste of food and of our precious time. So, by heightening the overall pH value, we may safely water bathe the jars at 212°F (100°C) for 25 minutes or process the jars in a pressure canner at 10 PSI for 10 minutes.

In this example, if we had not added additional acid, we would have needed to process the salsa in a water bath for 40 minutes or in a pressure canner for 25 minutes to accomplish the same result of shelf stability without the presence of foodborne pathogens and microorganisms.

WHAT ARE FOODBORNE PATHOGENS?

Foodborne pathogens are in the form of bacteria and viruses. There are several common foodborne pathogens we need to be mindful of whether we

Processing, Storage, and Bacteria Temperature Controls

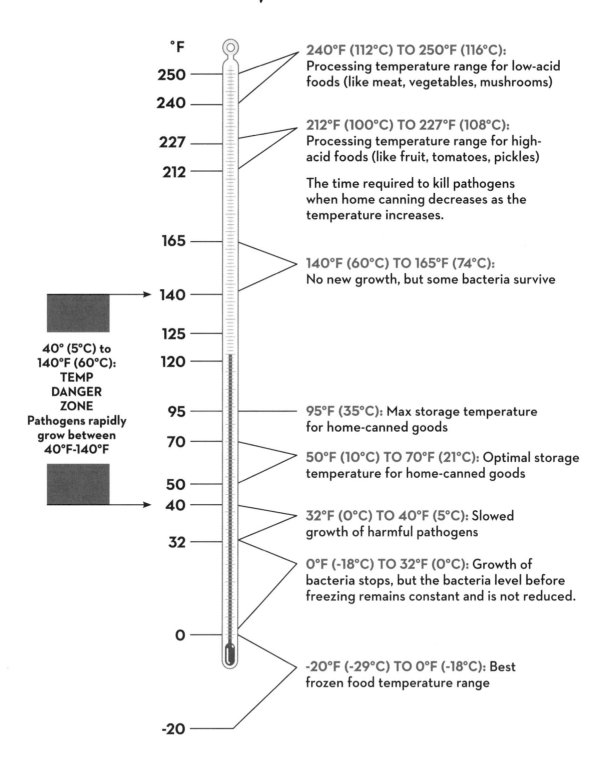

°F

240°F (112°C) TO 250°F (116°C):
Processing temperature range for low-acid foods (like meat, vegetables, mushrooms)

212°F (100°C) TO 227°F (108°C):
Processing temperature range for high-acid foods (like fruit, tomatoes, pickles)

The time required to kill pathogens when home canning decreases as the temperature increases.

140°F (60°C) TO 165°F (74°C):
No new growth, but some bacteria survive

40° (5°C) to 140°F (60°C): TEMP DANGER ZONE
Pathogens rapidly grow between 40°F-140°F

95°F (35°C): Max storage temperature for home-canned goods

50°F (10°C) TO 70°F (21°C): Optimal storage temperature for home-canned goods

32°F (0°C) TO 40°F (5°C): Slowed growth of harmful pathogens

0°F (-18°C) TO 32°F (0°C): Growth of bacteria stops, but the bacteria level before freezing remains constant and is not reduced.

-20°F (-29°C) TO 0°F (-18°C): Best frozen food temperature range

250
240
227
212
165
140
125
120
95
70
50
40
32
0
-20

are cooking or canning at home. While so much emphasis is placed on botulism, oftentimes, home canners fail to recognize there are more common contributors to food spoilage and illness than the rare occurrence of botulism. Here are the most common foodborne pathogens that spoil our food and make us sick:

- *Salmonella and Campylobacter:* Bacteria commonly found in raw or undercooked poultry, eggs, and meat.

- *E. coli*: A bacterium commonly found in undercooked ground beef and contaminated produce. Produce is often contaminated by infected humans handling food, by animal feces near the field, or by using an infected water source while growing or rinsing the crop after harvest. E. coli will penetrate the surface of the produce and cannot be rinsed off.

- *Listeria:* A bacterium found in ready-to-eat foods such as deli meats, soft cheese, and smoked fish. Listeria can thrive in a cold environment like the refrigerator.

- *Norovirus:* A virus commonly spread through contaminated food and water and contact with infected individuals. Noroviruses are the leading cause of foodborne illnesses such as food poisoning or other stomach bugs.

- *Clostridium botulinum:* A heat-resistant bacterium that produces a toxin grown only in anerobic environments. The toxin can be present underground in the soil when growing root crops like potatoes and carrots, and it could also be present in commercial and home-canned foods that have not been processed correctly.

The key to staying safe in the home kitchen is knowledge. Understanding what is harmful, from where it derives, and how to avoid it are the first steps in keeping your food and loved ones safe. So, what do we do to prevent these harmful pathogens from contaminating our food? Here is a quick list of how to procure, clean, and store foods prior to using them in canning recipes, greatly lessening the risk of contamination:

1. When grocery shopping, keep raw meat, poultry, and seafood separate from other foods in the grocery cart. I will often use the bottom rack of the cart for all raw meats and the basket for everything else.

2. Grow and raise your own food or rely on a reputable farmer or food source to procure your fresh produce, meat, eggs, poultry, and fish.

3. Properly and fully cook meat, poultry, eggs, and fish to their appropriate internal temperature to kill any bacteria present.

4. After use and prior to storing, clean surfaces and utensils with bleach or similar detergent and rinse well with hot running water.

5. Use clean running water to wash and scrub produce and use a vegetable brush to thoroughly clean root crops prior to use in any recipe.

6. Ensure your refrigerator is at or below the proper storage temperature of 40°F (4°C). I always keep my refrigerator temperature at 38°F (3°C).

7. Be certain your freezer is at or below 0°F (-18°C) and your deep freezer is at or below -13°F (-25°C).

8. When storing food at home, never place raw meat, poultry, and seafood on the shelf above other foods in the refrigerator. Always store them on the bottom shelf to keep any of their liquid from dripping onto fresh foods and produce.

WHAT ARE MICROORGANISMS?

Whether home canning or simply cooking food in your kitchen, microorganisms are a natural part of our existence. Microorganisms are all around us—in the soil, in the water, even in the air we breathe. Food-spoilage microorganisms are often grouped together as yeast, mold, and fungi.

Fungi are a broader group of organisms that includes yeast and mold as well as other organisms like mushrooms. Not all fungi are harmful to humans; however, some can cause food spoilage and foodborne illnesses. For instance, some fungi can produce toxins, like mycotoxins, that contaminate food and cause illness if consumed. Food types susceptible to mycotoxin contamination are grains, nuts, spices, dried fruits, and coffee beans.

Yeast is a type of fungus that can grow in foods, particularly those containing sugar, and can cause fermentation, leading to changes in flavor, texture, and appearance. While yeast can be beneficial in some instances, like baking bread and brewing beer, it will cause spoilage in other foods like fruit.

Mold is another type of fungus that will grow on foods such as bread, cheese, and fruit. Mold can cause spoilage by producing toxins that render food unsafe to eat. Worse, certain molds can cause allergic reactions in some people.

How to Avoid and Prevent Contamination

Microorganisms are living things that require certain conditions to grow and thrive. Optimal living conditions to thrive depend on moisture, an ideal temperature range between 60°F (15°C) and 90°F (32°C), and air, or free oxygen.

These three optimal conditions are why we've been taught from a young age to not let our leftovers sit on the countertop for too long. With any leftover food, we know we must cool it quickly, place it in an airtight container, and store it in the refrigerator promptly. We are also advised to eat our leftovers within a week to avoid consuming spoiled food. How many of us have forgotten a Tupperware container of leftovers in the back of the fridge and were grossed out by fuzzy green mold growing on last Tuesday's lasagna?

While refrigeration is a form of food preservation, using cold temperatures to delay food

spoilage is a short-term solution. Worse, those pesky microorganisms can also destroy our home-canned foods if we do not properly wash our hands, clean and prepare our food, and process canning recipes at the required time and temperature.

SIGNIFICANCE OF PROPER STORAGE CONDITIONS

Now that you have learned about the science and math behind home canning and have learned the harmful foodborne pathogens and microorganisms to avoid, it is vital to understand the significance of proper storage to ensure a long lifespan of your home-canned goods. Nothing is worse than investing all your time, energy, food, and money into creating and preserving delicious meals in a jar, only to have everything fail because careful consideration was not placed into the final stage of home canning: storage.

We all live differently and have different spaces within our homes for storing food. Many of us utilize a pantry. However, I understand not everyone has a dedicated pantry space. In these cases, we must create one. But to do so we must first ask ourselves, *What is a pantry?*

A pantry is a storage area where food, dishes, and other kitchen supplies are kept. The pantry may be a separate room or a closet-like space, preferably near the kitchen. For those of us with basements, the pantry is often created downstairs due to the naturally cooler temperatures. The purpose of a pantry is to provide additional storage space for nonperishable food items such as canned goods, boxed or bagged items like pasta, cereal, and snacks, and supplies like paper towels, toilet paper, and cleaning products.

A pantry can help keep the kitchen organized, and it can allow space to stock up on frequently used items or to store bulk purchases. In addition to providing storage space, a pantry can also help extend the shelf life of nonperishable food items by keeping them in a cool, dry, and dark environment. This can help reduce food waste and save money.

To help you locate the perfect storage space in your home, here are the optimal conditions for long-term storage of your home-canned goods:

- out of direct or indirect sunlight
- in a temperature range of 50°F (10°C) to 70°F (21°C)
- free from humidity and excess moisture
- away from vast temperature swings or appliances that generate heat
- elevated off dirt or cement floors
- with suitable shelf heights to avoid stacking jars atop one another

What areas of your home fit these conditions? While many of us gravitate to storing extra nonperishables in our kitchen, be sure to avoid cabinets above your refrigerator and stove since they generate heat and heat rises. Additionally, if the spare room you designate as your pantry has a window, be sure to use a blackout curtain or similar means to eliminate direct and indirect sunlight.

Last, there are many forgotten or unused spaces in the home that make perfect long-term storage solutions. Here are just a few:

- under beds
- hallway linen closets
- under stairwells
- spare bedroom closets
- unused cabinets away from appliances

A key element to remember when storing your home-canned goods is to store jars with the rings off. Doing so will help you detect a false seal and will immediately identify if a lid became unsealed during storage and spoiled the food. Simply remove the ring after the jars have cooled, wash your sealed jars in soapy water then rinse and dry each jar with a hand towel. Leaving the ring on the jar may cause moisture leading to rust and corrosion, making it a vein-popping experience to remove the ring from the jar.

Another key element to remember is to label the jar lid with the name of the recipe and the month and year it was canned. Doing so will help you properly rotate your food supply. It is imperative to consume the oldest food first and place recently canned jars in the back of the shelf to be consumed last. This practice is called *first in, first out.*

What Is the Shelf Life of Home-Canned Foods?

It is recommended we consume our home-canned goods within their first year because the food is at its optimal nutritional value. Consider this as a recommended "best by" date, not an expiration date. If it stays longer in storage, the food won't be unsafe to consume, but it will lose a portion of its nutritional value every year it is stored. This small amount of loss doesn't mean the foods have to be tossed after one year in storage. Here is what I tell all my students:

In a world where junk food is readily available and often consumed, knowing full well its nutritional value is ridiculously low to almost nonexistent, I am completely content consuming my home-canned recipes into their third, fourth, or even fifth year of storage with only half their nutritional value intact.

Why?

Because I know what I put into every jar. My food is not laden with chemicals I cannot pronounce. I prepared the recipes with my own two hands in my own kitchen. I grew, raised, or procured every ingredient for every recipe start to finish. Each lid remained sealed. And I have stored my home-canned foods in the proper storage conditions.

Now, you will also hear me say, "If you won't eat it, don't can it." So, while we are safe to consume our sealed home-canned goods years into storage, if food is sitting on your pantry shelf because you don't want to eat it, then you know not to ever can it again. In these cases, gift the items or pitch the food and reuse the jars. There's no need to give valuable pantry space to things you will not eat.

Getting Started

In this chapter you will learn about the essential canning supplies and tools to ensure your kitchen is prepped for canning and preserving food. It breaks down the types of pressure canners on the market, including digital canners, and contains a helpful guide to record your canner details, specifications, and elevation. Each canner operates using pressure; however, each manufacturer offers slight differences in the way their product is utilized. We will also spend some time learning how elevation plays a vital role in safe processing time, so no matter where you reside, you will be able to safely preserve low-acid foods.

In this chapter you will also be given the top ten rules of pressure canning to build your confidence to safely operate a pressure canner in your home kitchen. Further, we will explore the various types of stovetops and cooktops to help you decide which type of canner is right for you. We will dive into the four types of jar-packing methods used in home canning so you may learn their similarities and differences and assess how each method has its place among the plethora of canning recipes within each chapter.

Last, and most exciting, we will spend time together reviewing ways to efficiently plan your pressure-canning endeavors so you may maximize each growing and harvest season. There is a time investment when learning how to preserve food, so learning tips and techniques to prep your kitchen space and your busy schedule will make pressure canning so much more enjoyable in the end.

ESSENTIAL CANNING SUPPLIES

There's nothing worse than planning to preserve a meal in a jar only to realize you are missing important utensils to help you measure, ladle, or cook the recipe prior to processing. And yes, there are hundreds of cool gadgets and gizmos on the market, often creating confusion for the canner about which ones are actually necessary

and which are just "cool to have." I learned a long time ago that many of the tools included in utensil kits just take up space in my kitchen because they never get used. To help you avoid wasting kitchen space, here is a list of essential canning utensils to make your experience a positive one.

Canning Tools

Headspace-measuring and air pocket–remover tool: This inexpensive tool was created specifically for home canning. It allows us to measure the headspace required in each jar. It is long and flat with notched edges on one side bearing the etchings of measurements from ¼ inch to 1 inch. To measure headspace, you simply place the notched ledge with the recipe's required headspace measurement on the lip of the jar. When the food touches the tip of the tool, you know you have filled the jar properly.

Proper headspace is important to give the food room to swell and move without it escaping the jar. If there is too much food in a jar, the food will be pushed out during processing, causing the food to escape from the jar and into the canner vessel. There is also the risk of food getting on the jar rim, which could prevent the lid from sealing.

The opposite end of this handy tool doubles as an air pocket remover. When you are filling jars with a canning recipe, it is vital to release these trapped air pockets so you may maximize each jar's capacity and ensure proper headspace. Simply immerse the tool down into the jar along the outer edge and run it all the way around the jar's

interior to remove any trapped air pockets. It is common to then add additional food to return it to the correct headspace.

Wide-mouthed jar funnel: When filling the jars with a canning recipe, the funnel helps ensure each jar receives what is intended rather than the food being wasted because it missed getting into the jar. It also helps us keep the jar lids clean, saving us time and elbow grease when wiping a jar rim prior to adhering the lid and ring.

Cutting boards: Often our canning recipes are boiled prior to filling the jars. While a cutting board is used to prep ingredients, it is also the perfect solution to keep a hot glass jar away from a cold countertop surface. This is important to avoid shocking the bottom of a hot glass jar.

Even when raw packing cold ingredients into cold jars, we will often tap the jar onto the cutting board surface to release any trapped air pockets the headspace-measuring tool cannot reach. The cutting board lessens the impact, keeping our glass jars from obtaining impact fractures. Resting canning jars on a cutting board during packing is a great habit to create no matter the packing method.

Last, we will cover a cutting board with a dish towel to give our processed jars a safe place to cool. The dish towel acts as a buffer and absorbs the water from the jars.

An extra weighted gauge: It still amazes me how the lack of such a simple component like a weighted gauge can render a pressure canner completely useless. Without this weight, the pressure canner cannot build the pressure needed to increase the temperature past the boiling point. Every pressure canner comes with its own weight, however, if your weight goes missing, your plans for pressure canning are over until you find a new weight. To avoid this, always purchase a second weight and store it in a safe place so you are never without one.

Dish towels and terry cloth or microfiber washcloths: In my kitchen I love using crisp white dishcloths to match my decor. Home canning requires extra towels to keep things clean, but they also act as a buffer between a hot jar and a cooler surface. Red spaghetti sauce residue on my white dish towels would ruin them, so to avoid this, I have a separate set of dish towels from the dollar store set aside specifically for canning.

When it comes to washcloths, I have three dedicated to jar-rim wiping. Keeping these separate from your everyday-use kitchen washcloths ensures you are wiping your jar rims with something that didn't just wipe down your kitchen sink. We do not want to spread bacteria onto our jar rims; we want to rid the rims of it. Terry cloth and microfiber are the best substrate to remove any small particles or food debris from the jar rim.

Canning jars: There are so many new jar manufacturers on the market because, let's face it, mason jars are cool! We can make crafts with them, use them as cups for drinking, store stuff in them—you name it. But not every jar on the market is designed for home canning. Many are designed to *look* like mason jars but are built for decorative purposes. When you're shopping for glass jars, make sure the ones you purchase are designed for home-canning use.

Did you know canning jars are *not* made with tempered glass? Canning jars go through an annealing process, meaning they are thermally treated at 800°F (427°C) to 900°F (482°C) and then heat soaked until the temperature is consistent throughout the entire jar and it has the stress adequately reduced.

Canning lids: Lids are another important factor in home canning. Without superior lids, we can lose all our time, effort, and the food we made when a lid fails to seal. Sometimes this just happens; other times it is a result of a faulty canning lid.

In recent years, new manufacturers have emerged to fill the gaps in the market. While this may sound exciting, it has caused a great deal of pain for canners across the globe. Cheap knockoffs made of thin metal and limited, or inferior, sealing compound will ruin your canning experience and waste your food. Ensure you are purchasing one-time-use canning lids from a reputable source. The temporary savings may cost you more in the long run. Another option is to purchase reusable canning lids that mirror the rubber seal and plastic lid top from yesteryear. There have been many positive results from canners who use these BPA-free plastic lids, and they seem to really be growing in popularity.

Canning rings or screw bands: Canning rings, also called screw bands, are made of tin-plated steel. They are reusable and can be kept indefinitely so long as they have not become overly rusted. Before you know it, you will have hundreds of rings in storage. I have learned the hard way to hand-wash and air-dry my canning rings rather than tossing them in the dishwasher. Sadly, the detergent and extended washing time breaks them down much faster, causing them to rust quicker. Some manufacturers have made thicker, stamped stainless steel canning rings, which are impervious to rust and won't lose their shape. They come with a hefty price tag but will pay for themselves in the long run.

Permanent marker and labels: Labeling the jar lids with the name of the recipe and the month and year it was made is vital to proper food rotation in our pantries. Paper labels work great during storage but become harder to read when inked with a ballpoint pen. Use a permanent marker to keep the label intact for years.

Reliable timer: As you've already learned, processing time is a pillar that keeps us safe when home canning. Without a reliable timer, we could underprocess our canning recipes, causing our food to spoil or germinate harmful pathogens during storage. Overprocessing will cause our foods to taste burnt or render the food so mushy it is inedible. Having a reliable timer and starting it when the pressure canner reaches the required PSI will prevent each of these catastrophes.

Safety Tools

Waterproof, heat resistant mitts: Working around extreme temperatures is commonplace when home canning. To protect our hands while handling hot jars and boiling pots and working around the steam generated by a pressure canner, it is vital to wear protective mitts. I love my waterproof, heat resistant canning mitts so much that I use them to take the hot jars in and out of the pressure canner. Mitts also protect us from steam burns when we remove the pressure canner lid after processing. You will often find these amazing mitts at culinary or restaurant supply stores or online.

Jar-lifter tool: Most canning utensil kits come with this handy tool. If waterproof and heat resistant mitts are not in your budget, or are not available in your area, this handy tool makes removing jars from the pressure canner a cinch. Just be sure to use the tool properly. I often see canners using it upside down when grabbing the jars. Use the end that has the tacky grip coating of rubber or silicone, and not the plastic bars, to grab the hot jars. The plastic bars are for your hands.

Long apron with pockets: Let's face it, working in the kitchen can be messy. There are times I stand back after canning and swear someone let a bomb off in my kitchen. Additionally, working with boiling-hot substances can be dangerous. Moving stockpots from one burner to the next or emptying the canner water in the sink is a common occurrence when canning. Protect your clothing, your upper body, and your legs with a well-made apron. Look for models with adjustable neck straps and conveniently placed pockets, and ensure that your apron is long enough to protect your chest, abdomen, and upper legs.

Additional Canning Tools

Deep stockpots or a large Dutch oven: Canning a single-batch recipe will often yield seven quarts of food. Make sure you have a 24- or 32-quart stockpot handy. I frequently use my stainless steel 32-quart water bather when creating a pressure-canning recipe. Dutch ovens work well, especially if your canning recipe requires a long time to simmer or reduce prior to filling the jars.

If you happen to own two 23-quart stovetop pressure canners, you may use one to create the recipe and the other to preserve it. This was the solution I used when I had the pleasure of teaching Carrie Underwood and her friends, the Garden Gals, how to safely use a pressure canner. When we started prepping our ingredients, we quickly realized we needed a much larger pot to accommodate the triple batch of soup we were making. With three canners in tow, we used one canner to create the chicken soup and the other two canners were double stacked full of jars for processing. Just remember, the bigger the pot, the better when home canning!

Long-handled spoons: Both mixing spoons and slotted spoons are essential when home canning.

My Glass Coffeepot Analogy

Imagine you have friends over for coffee one morning. You reach for your glass coffeepot and graciously top off your friends' mugs with the last of the coffee. Would you then head straight to the sink and fill your glass coffeepot with ice-cold water to brew another batch? No, you sure wouldn't. Because you know doing so would likely crack or even shatter the glass coffeepot. A glass canning jar is no different.

Simply put, the temperature of the recipe determines the temperature of the glass and the temperature of the canner water. For example, if you are raw stacking a recipe with cold ingredients, the glass jar must be cool, or room temperature, and the canner water must also be cool or room temperature. The same is true in reverse: if the recipe being packed into the jar is boiling hot, the glass jar and canner water must also be hot. You may keep your jars hot by placing your jars in a quick-rinse cycle of your dishwasher and leaving them to sit there until you are ready to pack them. Another option is to keep your glass jars hot by submerging them in hot water in the sink.

Treat your glass canning jars like a glass coffeepot and you will avoid stress fractures and thermal shock. Doing so will give your glass canning jars many wonderful years of use.

The longer the handle, the better the ability to mix your ingredients in deep stockpots. Ensure the handle is long enough to allow you to avoid burning your hand while bringing ingredients up from the bottom of the pot, so you can properly heat through all the food and avoid scorching.

Long-handled slotted spoons are also essential because they allow us canners to pull solid ingredients from the stockpot and place them into the jars. This method of filling the jars with solids first allows us to control the ratio of solids to liquid when packing the jars. It ensures the first jar being filled doesn't wind up with all the solids while the last jar contains nothing but liquid and remnants of what was supposed to be a hearty soup.

Large ladle: Fill your jars faster and more efficiently by using a ladle with a large scoop on the end. The majority of canning recipes require you to ladle the recipe into a jar, so be certain you have one in your canning arsenal.

Vinegar and cream of tartar: Vinegar is your best friend in the kitchen, especially when you're home canning. Vinegar naturally kills bacteria and helps us keep our jars clean. When wiping the jar rims, dab a bit of vinegar on a terry cloth washcloth to help remove any debris, sugary residue, or grease. Those of us with well water will often have a cloudy white substance on our glass jars after canning. To prevent such mineral deposits from etching your glass jars, place one ounce of vinegar in the canner water prior to processing.

Like our jars, a pressure canner's interior will also show signs of buildup. To clean the interior of your pressure canner, add one tablespoon of cream of tartar to 4 cups of water. Bring it to a boil and cover the canner until the deposits disappear. This will also help remove the black marks often found at the base and side of its interior.

TYPES OF PRESSURE CANNERS

While there are different styles of pressure canners, each pressure canner is essentially the same in its function and, for the most part, its design. A pressure canner consists of a large pot with a lid that is designed to lock and seal tightly. Inside the pot, or vessel, there is a flat rack sitting on its base to elevate the jars off the bottom of the canner to avoid direct contact with the heat source. The vessel is filled with water up to a certain level, and then the jars are placed inside. The lid is secured, and heat is applied to the pot to generate steam.

Steam exhausts for a specific amount of time to remove cold spots and to ensure the vessel will be hot enough to build pressure. After it vents steam, a weight is placed on the vent pipe to prevent steam and heat from escaping. As the steam builds up inside the pot, it creates pressure, which is regulated by a weight, dial, or sensor.

Once the canner reaches the desired pressure, the heat is turned down to maintain the pressure and temperature for the required amount of time. After the processing time is complete, the heat is turned off, and the canner is left to cool down naturally. As the canner cools, the pressure inside decreases until there is no more pressure in the vessel and we may remove the canner lid and lift out the jars.

There are two different types of pressure canners: stovetop canners and digital electric canners. The stovetop models offer two different types, a weighted gauge canner and a dial gauge canner. The digital electric canners suited for pressure canning low-acid foods have digital controls and a unique venting system, and they plug into a standard electrical outlet.

The main difference between each of these canners is the way they regulate pressure. In a dial-gauge canner, the pressure inside the canner is measured by a pressure dial, or a needle within the gauge, attached to the lid. The needle points to the PSI. This allows the user to monitor and adjust the pressure as needed during the canning process. A weighted gauge canner does not have a dial and relies solely on the use of the weight. It is designed to allow steam to escape at a specific pressure range, typically 5, 10, or 15 PSI.

Dial gauge canners may require periodic calibration to ensure the pressure gauge is accurate. This is because the gauge can become inaccurate over time due to wear and tear, which can lead to under- or overprocessing the food. Some manufacturers sell a calibration unit with instructions so you can test your dial gauge at home. On the other hand, a weighted gauge canner does not require calibration because the weighted regulator is designed to release steam at a specific pressure range indicated by the weight itself.

What Is the Difference Between a Pressure Cooker and a Pressure Canner?

Technically a pressure cooker operates exactly as a pressure canner does, creating a high-pressure, high-temperature environment inside its vessel. The difference, however, is a pressure cooker is manufactured to cook food quickly, is built smaller in size, and typically operates at a lower PSI. Yes, it is true that a pressure cooker will achieve 15 PSI, or 250°F (121°C). However, it will fluctuate from 8 PSI to 15 PSI and there is no way to consistently regulate or control it. Pressure canners give us the ability to regulate the PSI consistently for long periods of time and are much larger in size. A pressure canner has the capacity to hold multiple jars at once, often with the ability to double stack jars, producing a higher yield.

Digital canners operate very differently, as pressure and temperature are monitored and controlled using sensors and electric heating elements. Although newer to the marketplace, digital canners provide greater temperature precision and control and plug into a standard electrical outlet, taking up no stove space.

All three types of pressure canners operate on the same principle of creating a high-pressure environment inside the canner. Let's look more closely at the differences in the way they each regulate pressure.

Weighted gauge canners rely on a tight-locking lid and a weight. Depending on the manufacturer, a series of three separate weights in the amounts of 5 PSI, 10 PSI, and 15 PSI may be offered, or it could be a single weight with three different markers indicated by drilled holes for specific placement onto the vent pipe to obtain the three different pounds of pressure. Some manufacturers will provide a mechanism to combine three separate 5 PSI weights to achieve the desired pounds of pressure.

The weight is calibrated to rock back and forth as the pressure inside the canner fluctuates, which helps to regulate the pressure using the stovetop burner knob to control the heat output, therefore maintaining a consistent temperature throughout the canning process. It makes a gentle ticking sound so you can hear it and see it rocking. This rocking motion is why many will call the weighted gauge a *jiggler*.

Dial gauge canners rely on a visual indicator by way of the PSI dial resting on top of the canner lid. As the canner heats up and builds pressure, the needle will rise and indicate the PSI within the vessel. Like the weighted gauge canner, once the vessel has reached the required PSI, you use the stovetop burner knob to reduce the heat to maintain the pressure. When using a dial gauge canner, the PSI is often higher in canning recipes. For instance, at zero elevation, a canning recipe specifying processing at 10 PSI for a weighted gauge canner will often require 11 PSI for a dial gauge canner. A dial gauge canner offers a more precise pressure reading than a weighted gauge canner, allowing for more accurate control, and can also operate at a higher pressure range than its counterpart.

Both styles come in different sizes. I recommend purchasing a 15-quart canner or larger. I personally use a tall 23-quart canner and purchase a second flat rack so I may double stack my pint jars and half-pint jars. Doing so helps you process more jars at a time.

Digital electric pressure canners use an electric heating element to generate heat, which is then regulated by a thermostat to maintain a consistent temperature throughout the entire processing time. Its vessel has sensors that monitor the pressure inside the canner, allowing it to adjust the heating element as needed to maintain the desired pressure.

The touch screen controls, or control knob, allow you to designate the amount of time you wish to process. After walking through a series of steps, including the placement of its unique gauge to close the vent pipe, a digital canner does not require that we tend to it as we would with a stovetop canner. After processing, the digital pressure canner has a cooling cycle that will sound an alarm to indicate the pressure is at zero and it is safe to remove the canner lid.

Digital canners are not as large as stovetop canners, so they fit fewer jars. Many canners don't mind the smaller size because they will often cut a canning recipe in half to produce a smaller batch more suitable for their needs. Also, with digital canners, you cannot double stack your jars like you can with a stovetop canner. I know many canners who purchase two digital canners to combat these differences and will operate them simultaneously when canning large-scale recipes.

HOW YOUR STOVETOP PLAYS A ROLE

A great deal of how we decide which pressure canner to purchase is based on the type of stovetop or cooktop we have in our home kitchens. Pressure canners are made from either aluminum, cast aluminum, or stainless steel. Let's review the various types of cooktops so you can decide which style canner is right for you.

Gas stovetops and cooktops will use either liquid propane or natural gas. They are considered the most suitable for home canning because they provide more precise temperature control and faster heat-up times. When pressure canning, it is important to maintain a consistent and accurate temperature to ensure proper processing. Gas stoves and cooktops offer this precision as the heat output can be adjusted instantly with almost immediate results. This is important when monitoring the PSI and needing to increase or decrease the pressure.

Also keep in mind the burner output, or BTU, when using gas in the home. Use a burner with a higher output of 12,000 BTU and not less than 8,100 BTU to produce enough heat to operate your pressure canner. However, if the BTU output exceeds 12,000 BTU, you run the risk of warping the bottom of your canner, causing it to bulge, and rendering it unusable. The best canners for

gas stoves and cooktops are thick-bottomed pressure canners or pressure canners made from cast aluminum.

Electric stoves and cooktops have a couple of different varieties. Some offer electric coiled burners, others have flat glass tops with the electric heating element placed under the glass. When the burner is turned on, an electric current flows through the metal coil, which has a high resistance to the flow of electricity. This resistance causes the metal coil to heat up, and as it heats up, it radiates heat to the cookware placed on top of it. This function can lead to slower heating times and less-precise temperature control. You will notice this when you turn your stovetop control knob down to reduce the heat on the burner and it takes a while for the pressure canner to respond. This leads to a great deal more time spent tending to your pressure canner to regulate the heat, but it's nothing you cannot overcome once you get used to operating your pressure canner.

Flat glass electric stoves and cooktops work in a similar way, but instead of a metal coil, they have a heating element located beneath a smooth glass surface. These models generally take longer to heat up, and the glass surface is susceptible to cracking. Once a pressure canner is filled with its required level of water and jars full of food, the pressure canner can get very heavy. Some cast-aluminum pressure canners can weigh upwards of 20 pounds before a single jar is placed inside them. Consult the stove or cooktop manufacturer user guide to ensure you do not exceed any weight limits given for your flat glass-top model or call

Know Your Canner

Use this handy chart to record information about your pressure canner, giving you a simple reference point every time you preserve delicious home-canned meals in a jar.

Brand (Presto, Mirro, All American, etc.):

_____

Type (weighted, dial, or digital):

_____

Amount of water required (3 quarts, etc.):

_____

Vent time (10 minutes, etc.):

_____

My elevation:

_____

My required PSI for low-acid recipes
(10 PSI, 15 PSI):

_____

wire located beneath the surface of the cooktop. This creates a rapidly changing magnetic field, which in turn induces an electric current in the cookware placed on top of the cooktop. The electric current heats up the cookware directly rather than heating up the cooktop and transferring the heat to the cookware. This process is called electromagnetic induction, and it is what makes induction cooktops more energy efficient than traditional gas or electric cooktops.

Induction cooktops are also very precise in their heating, as the heat is generated directly in the cookware and can be controlled by adjusting the strength of the magnetic field. Only certain types of metal are compatible with induction cooktops because they need to be able to generate an electrical current when exposed to a magnetic field. Generally, the best types of metal to use on an induction cooktop are ferrous metals, which include:

- cast iron
- stainless steel with a magnetic grade (look for the "induction compatible" label)
- enameled steel
- some types of carbon steel

Nonferrous metals, such as aluminum, copper, and nonmagnetic stainless steel, will not work on an induction cooktop unless they have a layer on the bottom that is made of a ferromagnetic material. Some cookware manufacturers produce hybrid cookware that has a magnetic layer added to the base of noncompatible metals to make them induction compatible.

the manufacturer and inquire if your model is suitable for pressure canning.

Induction stovetops and cooktops work by using an electromagnetic field to directly heat the cookware. When the cooktop is turned on, an alternating electric current flows through a coil of

While stovetop canners are the most-used pressure canner by home canners, the digital electric canners are rising in popularity. Digital pressure canners are chosen for a variety of reasons, including the type of stovetop or cooktop owned. Some of us may choose a digital canner to keep our stovetop space free no matter its burner type because a digital canner can be operated while it sits on the countertop.

When I purchased a new home, I inherited an electric glass-top stove, which has limited me greatly. Electric stoves are built to cycle their power on and off during the cooking process, which can make it more difficult to bring large vessels to a rapid boil. This cycling of heat means it may not have enough power to bring a 23-quart pressure canner to a boil, let alone maintain a required PSI. Sadly, I was not able to bring even a water bath to a full rolling boil. For this reason, I purchased a digital pressure canner to use in my kitchen.

UNDERSTANDING ALTITUDE WHEN PRESSURE CANNING

Altitude can have a significant effect on pressure canning because it affects the boiling point of water. At higher altitudes, the atmospheric pressure is lower, which means that the pressure inside the canner needs to be higher in order to achieve the same temperature as at sea level. Therefore, for people who live at higher altitudes, a dial gauge or digital canner may be more suitable, as it can adjust to the higher pressure requirements to keep our food safe.

When pressure canning, we know it is important to reach a certain temperature to kill harmful pathogens and microorganisms that cause illness and food spoilage. We also learned a pressure canner must reach and maintain a specific pressure and temperature for a set amount of time to achieve this. However, at higher altitudes, the boiling point of water is lower, which means it will take longer to reach the required temperature.

To compensate for this, the pressure required for pressure canning in higher altitudes is increased. Its required increase depends on the altitude and the type of food being canned. It is recommended you add an additional 1 PSI of pressure for every 2,000 feet above sea level. Keep in mind only the PSI changes due to elevation. The processing time remains the same regardless of your altitude. To determine your altitude, you may use a free smartphone app with GPS or barometric pressure, a topographic map, an online altitude finder, or you may purchase a handheld altimeter.

ELEVATION GUIDE

Feet Above Sea Level	Weighted Gauge Canner (PSI)	Dial Gauge Canner (PSI)
0-1,000	10	11
1,001-2,000	15	11
2,001-3,000	15	12
3,001-6,000	15	13
6,001-8,000	15	14
8,001-10,000	15	15

June

Wednesday	Thursday	Friday	Saturday

Garden Plants
1. tomatoes
2. bell peppers
3. cabbage
4. potatoes
5. green beans

Herbs
1. parsley   2. cilantro
3. basil   4. mint

Plant Soil

Tomatoes - Roma

Beans

JAR PACKING METHODS

I love the fun of canning with my friends but generally I am canning alone in my own kitchen. Using what I learned from having many hands at my disposal, over the years I have developed quite an efficient process for working alone. The assembly-line style of jar packing really saves time getting the jars filled and in the canner quickly. And the best way to navigate any pressure-canning recipe is to understand and utilize the four jar-packing methods. They are raw packing, hot packing, dry packing, and raw stacking. Let's break them down together.

Raw Packing Method

This method is most suitable for vegetables, fruit, and root crops and also when pickling. Raw packing is the practice of filling jars tightly with fresh, uncooked food. Hence the term raw. When using this method, it is common to see foods, especially fruit, floating in the jars. The reason foods may float is due to trapped oxygen within the food's fibers, but this is natural and expected.

Hot Packing Method

Hot packing is the practice of heating freshly prepared food to boiling, simmering it for a specified length of time, and then filling the jars with the boiled food. Hot packing is the best way to remove air trapped within the food and is the preferred packing method for soups, stews, and thick sauces. Removing the trapped air, or preshrinking, allows us to better maximize the jar space and allows us to blend or reduce ingredients so the overall recipe is more concentrated and tastes more robust.

Every canning recipe written is based on sea-level elevation, which is considered 0 to 1,000 feet (0 to 305 meters) above sea level.

This is why each recipe throughout this book states, "Process in a pressure canner at 10 PSI or according to your elevation and canner type." The reason I state "canner type" is because some digital canner models do not permit you to select a PSI as they are pre-programmed to process at 240°F (116°C) no matter where you live. And "according to your elevation" is a reminder to consult our handy Elevation Guide on page 37 or the Know Your Canner chart on page 36 so you remember what adjustments to PSI you need to make.

Dry Packing Method

Dry packing is a method typically used when canning root crops such as potatoes as well as meat, poultry, and fish. As with traditional raw packing, the jar is tightly packed with food to maximize its yield. However, with dry packing, the food is not covered with boiling water. Instead, the food is often coated with a barrier of oil or fat such as ghee, butter, or extra-virgin olive oil. Doing so prevents enzymic browning, which is an oxidation reaction, and prevents the food from becoming dry. Enzymic browning is a natural occurrence when foods are exposed to air and it will not affect the food's safety.

Raw Stacking Method

Raw stacking is essentially raw packing by evenly distributing a tested ratio of ingredients and layering (stacking) them onto one another in the jar. We then cover the ingredients with a liquid, usually water, broth, or stock, then process the jars. We create a tested ratio of solids, seasonings, and liquid to yield a positive, safe, and delicious result. I have dedicated an entire chapter to using the raw stacking method (chapter 4).

PLAN YOUR PRESSURE CANNING

Home canning is a labor of love. Each of us puts a great deal of time into planning, preparing, and processing our canning recipes. In this book I have included an estimated prep time, cook time, and processing time for each canning recipe so you may efficiently plan your time.

It is common for a pressure-canning recipe to take upwards of four hours to complete, depending on its list of ingredients, its complexity, the desired yield, and of course, the processing time. Often, I will double or triple a canning recipe so I may "put up" as many jars as possible in one sitting. I mean, if you are willing to set aside 4 hours for a single batch, what's one more hour to triple the output? Many of us agree, if you're doing it anyway, you might as well go like gangbusters!

One way to lessen the load is to have friends or family join you in the fun. As the old saying goes: many hands make light work. Working together will greatly lessen the time it takes to prep ingredients, cook the recipe, and fill the jars. I will often get together with three or four girlfriends and rent a local commercial kitchen so we may create an assembly-line production type of setting to really crank out the jars. At the end of our six-hour session, there's nothing more satisfying than hearing the sound of 150 lids sealing. We then divvy up the jars and enjoy going home to clean kitchens.

Create a Personal Canning Calendar

Another way to be efficient in the kitchen is to map out and create your personal canning calendar. Whether you grow your own vegetables and fruit, have a homestead and raise your own protein, or simply shop at the grocery store, having a canning calendar truly helps you plan for the upcoming year's canning season.

A canning calendar is a dedicated road map based on your specific needs, which are dependent on where you live, your regional climate and seasons, and your personal eating habits. No two calendars will look alike because we eat differently, grow differently, and live in different parts of the world. To help streamline the process and create a canning calendar specific to your needs, here are tips to get you started:

1. Toward the end of the year, purchase next year's monthly calendar with enough space for writing notes and daily details.

2. In a notebook, take inventory of what you like to eat. Break it into categories for breakfast,

Top 10 Rules of Pressure Canning

1. Treat your glass jars like you would a glass coffeepot! Avoid vast temperature swings when working with glass.

2. Keep the vent pipe clean and free from debris. The vent pipe must be able to adequately exhaust steam. Hold the canner lid up to the light. If you do not see light through the vent hole, it is dirty and must be cleaned with hot running water and mild detergent.

3. Consult your manual for the proper venting time. The canner must adequately vent prior to processing. The most common venting time is 10 minutes.

4. Add one ounce of vinegar to the canner water prior to adding the jars for processing. Doing so will keep mineral deposits off your canning jars.

5. Use a reliable timer to avoid under- or overprocessing your food in the jars. And do not start your timer until your stovetop pressure canner has reached the required processing PSI.

6. Do not ever let your stovetop pressure canner's PSI get below the required PSI. If you're using a dial gauge pressure canner, going over the required PSI by 2 to 3 PSI is okay, but you must never go below it. If the PSI gets below the required amount, you will need to reprocess the jars.

7. Always let your pressure canner drop to zero pounds of pressure before removing the lid. Rushing this process could cause injury to you and your jars.

8. Once you are permitted to remove the canner lid, allow the jars to sit for a minimum of 5 minutes in the pressure canner before removing the jars to cool on a towel-lined cutting board on the countertop.

9. Food within the jars stays hot and active during cooling. Do not disturb the jars while they cool or you could prevent the second phase of thermal processing.

10. When using a digital canner that doubles as a water bather, be sure you have selected the proper pressure-canning setting to process low-acid foods.

lunch, dinner, snack, and dessert. Have fun by getting the kids involved so their food likes are also included.

3. Review the chapters in my cookbooks to start identifying canning recipes that will coordinate with what you eat in each category.

4. Once the recipes are determined, break down the variety of ingredients used within each recipe per category. You will start to see a pattern of ingredients arise. Highlight those patterns and use sticky notes to flag the canning recipe pages.

5. Take inventory of your shopping habits and purchases by reviewing the food in your pantry, cupboards, refrigerator, freezers, and storage areas to identify commonly purchased food products. Identify foods to preserve and add to your canning calendar. Identify ingredients already on hand you may use to create recipes identified in step 3.

6. Locate your growing zone so you know when the predominant ingredients are due to be harvested in your specific area. Use agricultural resources in your area for support if you do not grow or raise the ingredients yourself. Use the local grocery store's seasonal specials to identify when something will be readily available and on sale. (An example would be corned beef. This is a traditional meat consumed around Saint Patrick's Day in March. After the holiday, corned beef is on sale to clear out space for the next holiday special.)

7. After learning when ingredients are readily available in your area, open your canning calendar and begin to mark down when you want to buy certain ingredients. Next, write the names of the canning recipes you wish to preserve that month. Some harvest seasons may span two to three months, so be sure to divide up the food type and canning recipes accordingly.

8. Continue these notations throughout the calendar until you have exhausted your list of canning recipes and food types.

9. When you are ready to begin canning, look a month ahead and start scheduling your canning time around your personal and professional schedule. This is also a great opportunity to reach out to friends and family to set a date for a canning party.

To help you visualize creating your personal canning calendar, let's quickly run through the instructions using real ingredients and recipes.

Let's say you and your spouse really love eating chile rellenos, Bolognese sauce, and beef fajitas. You are pleased to find each of these recipes listed in this book. After reviewing the list of ingredients, you quickly see that all three recipes require tomatoes, and two of the recipes require peppers (poblano and bell peppers, respectively). While going through this exercise, you note the many aluminum cans of vegetables you buy at the store, including large quantities of diced canned tomatoes.

Next, you review your growing zone and look through sales fliers from your local grocer. You even start following a business page of a local farm stand on social media. Throughout your research, you are pleased to learn that tomatoes come into season in your area from late July to early September.

So what's next? Using all of the information you've gathered, it is now time to start mapping things out in your personal canning calendar. Starting in the month of July, you write the word "tomatoes" in the notes, and you write it again in the months of August and September. Because so many of your recipes require tomatoes, you decide to spread out your canning intentions between the three months.

In the notes for the month of July, you write "chile rellenos" and "Bolognese" for August, then you write "beef fajitas" in the notes for the month of September. You and your spouse are also huge fans of traditional salsa and really want to make your own tomato chutney during tomato season. So you jot those two water bath recipes down in the notes, one in the month of July and one in August. You continue to do this for each food type and canning recipe you wish to preserve throughout the year.

Fast-forward to the month before tomatoes come in season. At the start of June, you may now review your personal and professional schedule to learn what days and nights you will have free in July to create and preserve your recipes.

It's that easy! You simply build out your personal canning calendar using information you already know about yourself, how you eat, what you eat, and where you procure your foods. Yes, of course, you will find new recipes along the way, and you may even fit in a canning session or two when a food type is not in season. I often have to do this because the meal in a jar I created was consumed faster than I anticipated! It is not uncommon for me to preserve my kids' favorites multiple times throughout the year because I cannot keep them on the pantry shelf long enough.

And, by all means, do not wait until the start of a new year if you wish to begin canning recipes now. Use these same concepts and instructions any time of the year to start planning. Using a personal canning calendar to plan your water bathing and pressure canning endeavors will alleviate stress and help you capitalize on the opportunities to obtain the freshest ingredients while stretching your budget. Not to mention, it will help you stock your pantry in no time!

Ingredient Substitutions

Welcome to a chapter that will take your preservation journey to a whole new level! In this chapter we will unlock the art of ingredient substitution and recipe customization within the realm of pressure canning. Whether you're driven by health concerns, food allergies, or simply a desire to infuse your recipes with personal flair, I am here to guide you on a thrilling expedition of taste and creativity with safety at the forefront.

Canning, once a time-honored tradition for preserving the harvest, has evolved into a vibrant assortment of flavors and possibilities. While we respect the timeless wisdom of the USDA canning guidelines, I believe every individual should have the freedom to tailor recipes—within reason—to their own unique needs and desires. My mission is to empower you to break free from the confines of standardization and explore a world of delicious alternatives so you may enjoy the fruits of your labor (pun totally intended).

After digesting the information in this chapter, I hope you will gain a sense of confidence and autonomy in the kitchen. I want you to explore and experiment with ingredients and techniques while still being mindful of the Three Pillars of home canning shared in chapter 1 (page 15).

This chapter details the science and math behind food substitutions. I will delve into the intricacies of ingredient swaps, providing you with the tools to navigate this craft with pride and satisfaction.

I will dissect each element, examining the role of acids, liquids, and fats in achieving the perfect balance of taste and texture, while explaining the boundaries we must not cross. Armed with this knowledge, you'll be able to make informed decisions when substituting ingredients, ensuring your creations remain safe, delicious, and shelf stable.

SALT AND SUGAR SUBSTITUTIONS

The Skinny on Salt

Salt, chemically known as sodium chloride (NaCl), is an essential mineral that plays a vital role in human life. At the forefront, salt is essential to maintaining the balance of electrolytes in the body that are necessary for proper cellular function, muscle contraction, blood pressure regulation, digestion and absorption of nutrients, bodily fluid balance, and nerve transmission. However, excessive salt intake can have a negative effect on health, especially for individuals with certain medical conditions.

When pressure canning low-acid foods, salt is not used to preserve the food—it is merely included for taste and flavor. Adding salt to your meals in a jar enhances the taste and palatability of the food. When pressure canning low-acid recipes, we rely on time and temperature to safely preserve the food. However, when preserving acidic recipes, like salsa and pickles, salt is required to help inhibit bacterial growth. Let's break it down, shall we?

Sodium is a component of salt represented by the symbol Na on the periodic table. It is an essential mineral required by the body for proper functioning and it is an electrolyte that helps regulate the balance of fluids in the body. The terms *salt* and *sodium* are often used interchangeably, but they refer to different aspects. While sodium is a specific element, salt is the compound that contains sodium as one of its components.

Throughout the recipe chapters, you probably noticed that I include salt, or a sodium like soy sauce, in my recipes. You may also have noticed that, in most cases, I deem salt as an optional ingredient. This means if you are watching your salt intake, or if you prefer to season your individual portion of food later, you may omit the salt altogether. However, there are some recipes without the option to omit the salt or sodium. This is intentional because by omitting it from these recipes, they will no longer achieve the intended flavor profile, rendering the recipe tasteless or possibly off-putting.

So, what are your options for substituting salt or sodium when pressure canning meals in a jar? My personal and tested favorite is the use of coconut aminos as a viable and safe substitution for salt.

Coconut Aminos. This popular alternative to soy sauce is made from the fermented sap of coconut blossoms and has a savory, umami flavor like soy sauce. Coconut aminos typically undergo a natural fermentation process that contributes to its unique flavor. Although coconut aminos do contain sodium, the sodium content is generally lower compared to regular soy sauce or traditional table salt.

The reason I do not recommend a low-sodium version of soy sauce in my recipes is it may contain other additives or flavor enhancers to maintain a flavor similar to regular soy sauce. In certain cases, potassium chloride may be used as a partial or complete substitute for sodium chloride, which is regular salt. Consuming excessive amounts of potassium may not be suitable for individuals with certain medical conditions.

Citrus. Another option canners have are natural salt substitutes. Citrus, like lemon, lime, and orange, provide a tangy taste that can mimic the effect of salt. You can use fresh citrus juices, zest, or grated peel. Citrus-based seasoning contains dried citrus extracts or natural flavors to achieve a desired flavor profile without the need for salt. You will see a variety of citrus included in my recipes, such as whole dried limes common in Middle Eastern cuisine and fresh lemons used in Mediterranean cuisine.

Vinegars. Various types of vinegars, such as apple cider vinegar, balsamic vinegar, rice vinegar, and red wine vinegar, can contribute to the recipe's tanginess and depth of flavor. If you choose to add a vinegar to replace salt, bear in mind the change it will bring to the intended flavor profile of the recipe. In my recipes you will see the use of a variety of these vinegars included in Asian cuisine and in Mexican cuisine.

Yeast Extracts. Some salt substitutes use yeast extracts, such as nutritional yeast, to provide a savory and slightly salty taste. These extracts contain naturally occurring glutamates, which contribute to umami flavors. Using yeast extracts as a salt replacement may change the intended flavor profile of the recipe, especially depending on the brand purchased. While the yeast itself is denatured in this substitute, its cheese-like, nutty flavor profile may not work for every recipe.

Overall, the skinny on adding or omitting salt in low-acid pressure-canning recipes is a personal preference. If you are looking to use a salt substitute, be sure to start gingerly and taste as you go.

Revising the framework of a recipe's flavor profile could have a significantly negative effect on its taste and your enjoyment.

Sugar and Sweetening: Two Sides of the Coin

Sugar is a class of carbohydrates commonly used as a sweetener in various foods and beverages. Chemically, sugar refers to a group of organic compounds known as saccharides, which are made up of carbon, hydrogen, and oxygen atoms. The most common type of sugar is sucrose, which is extracted from sugar cane or sugar beets. Sucrose is a disaccharide composed of two simpler sugar units: glucose and fructose.

Sugar plays a variety of roles in food beyond providing sweetness. It can enhance flavors, improve texture, and contribute to the browning and caramelization of certain foods during cooking. In the context of pressure-canning recipes, sugar is often used to balance flavors, enhance taste, or provide a desirable sweetness to the preserved foods. It is important to note the primary purpose of sugar in pressure-canning recipes is for flavor rather than preservation.

There is a delicate balance, however, when incorporating granulated sugar into pressure-canning recipes. The excessive temperatures and lengthy processing time can negatively affect the outcome of the sugar added. If you add too much sugar, the recipe could have a burnt or scorched taste. Too little sugar, and the recipe's intended flavor profile may be amiss. However, adding sugar to some recipes can help offset an acidic flavor. For example, when using a higher ratio of tomatoes or when incorporating tomato paste, sugar helps *tone down* the overall acidic flavor, providing a more balanced and palatable experience.

Other times, you will see the use of brown sugar in my canning recipes. Brown sugar also contains sucrose along with varying amounts of molasses. It has a moist texture and a slightly sticky consistency thanks to the molasses. While granulated sugar has a neutral sweetness without any distinctive flavor notes, brown sugar has a richer and deeper flavor profile that offers a subtle hint of caramel or toffee-like taste, which can enhance the overall flavor of the canning recipe. Depending on the degree of molasses content, ranging from light to dark, the depth of the brown sugar will also enhance the recipe's flavor and deepen its color.

Using Food as a Sugar Substitute

Throughout each recipe chapter, you will see a wide variety of foods used to replicate the sweetness of sugar, without having to add granulated or brown sugar. I purposely chose to decrease the sugar content and increase the recipe's overall nutritional value.

For instance, several recipes instruct you to caramelize onions prior to adding additional ingredients. This is a culinary technique used to bring out the food's natural sugar content, which deepens the recipe's flavor and color. Dried fruit, fresh fruit, fruit juices, and naturally sweet vegetables like sweet potatoes and carrots can enhance the sweetness of a recipe without relying on added sugar. When you see these types of foods used in my canning recipes, know they are chosen to provide the recipe with the right amount of natural sweetness.

Sugar Substitutes That Are Safe for Home Canning

Excessive consumption of sugar, particularly refined sugars, has been associated with various health concerns, including obesity, type 2 diabetes, and dental issues. Therefore, many individuals consume sugar in moderation and choose to use healthier alternatives when possible.

There are some sugar alternatives that are heat tolerant and safe for use in pressure canning.

BROWN SUGAR SUBSTITUTES CHART

Brown Sugar Substitutes	1 cup		½ cup		¼ cup	
	Light	Dark	Light	Dark	Light	Dark
Molasses	1 T.	2 T.	1 tsp.	2 tsp.	½ tsp.	1 tsp.
Coconut Sugar	1 cup		½ cup		¼ cup	
Maple Syrup	¾ cup; reduce recipe's liquid by 3 T.		6 T.		3 T.	

WHITE SUGAR SUBSTITUTE CHART

Sugar Substitute per:	1 cup	½ cup	⅓ cup	¼ cup	3 T.	2 T.	1 T.
Agave sweetener	⅔ cup; reduce recipe's liquid by 2 T.	⅓ cup	¼ cup	2 T. + 2 tsp.	2 T.	1 T. + 1 tsp.	2 tsp.
Erythritol	1 cup	½ cup	⅓ cup	¼ cup	3 T.	2 T.	1 T.
Honey	¾ cup; reduce recipe's liquid by 3 T.	6 T.	4 T.	3 T.	2 T. + 1 tsp.	1 T. + 1 tsp.	2¼ tsp.
Maple syrup	¾ cup; reduce recipe's liquid by 3 T.	6 T.	4 T.	3 T.	2 T. + 1 tsp.	1 T. + 1 tsp.	2¼ tsp.
Monk fruit sweetener	½ cup	¼ cup	2 T.	2 to 3 T.	1 to 2 T.	1 T.	1½ tsp.
Splenda	½ cup	¼ cup	2 T. + 2 tsp.	⅛ cup	1 T. + ½ tsp.	1 T.	1½ tsp.
Stevia powder	1 tsp. or ½ tsp. liquid	½ tsp. or ¼ tsp. liquid	⅓ tsp. or scant ¼ tsp. liquid	¼ tsp. or scant ¼ tsp. liquid	¼ tsp. or a few drops liquid	⅛ tsp. or a few drops liquid	1/16 tsp. or 2 drops liquid

But there is a catch: many sugar substitutes are not in granulated form, so canners struggle to convert the recipe's measurements without under- or over-sweetening the recipe. Worse, some sugar alternatives and sweeteners may be lower in sucrose but are extremely sweet, which could potentially ruin the recipe's flavor.

These handy conversion charts can help you find a suitable sugar substitute when pressure canning.

When it comes to replacing sugar in a pressure-canning recipe, there are several things to take note of to ensure you achieve the best results. Substitutes like agave sweetener, honey, and maple syrup all increase the liquidity of the recipe. To compensate for that, you must slightly reduce the liquid in the canning recipe or allow the recipe to simmer for an additional 5 minutes to evaporate some of the liquid prior to filling the jars. Also, maple syrup and honey have distinctly different flavors compared to white granulated sugar, which could slightly alter the intended flavor profile of the recipe.

Substitutes like Splenda and stevia must be carefully used when pressure canning because of their overly sweet flavor. Splenda is 600 times sweeter than sugar and absorbs a great deal of liquid from the recipe. Stevia is highly concentrated, making it much sweeter than sugar, and it has an entirely different flavor from sugar, creating an unpleasant aftertaste if too much is used. Too much of either of these sugar substitutes can totally ruin the recipe, so less is always more.

Erythritol is a sugar alcohol that is roughly 70 percent as sweet as sugar. It has a similar sweetness profile and texture to sugar but with fewer calories and a lower glycemic impact. Keep in mind that erythritol produces a minty or cooling sensation when used in large quantities, so it is not recommended for canning recipes that require several cups of sugar.

If you are interested in omitting brown sugar from a pressure-canning recipe to avoid the high sucrose, there are safe and delicious substitutions. Use the chart on page 48 with measurements to aide you in substituting brown sugar in pressure-canning recipes.

Dark and medium molasses boasts a warm, sweet, and smoky flavor. Blackstrap molasses, however, is bitter in flavor and is not a good substitute for brown sugar. Coconut sugar is rich in flavor, boasting caramel notes, and is the most similar in flavor to brown sugar. Maple syrup has a similar flavor profile to brown sugar yet has

higher liquidity, so adjustments to the recipe's overall liquidity need to be made.

HERBS AND SPICES

When preserving low-acid recipes in a pressure canner, we have a great deal of flexibility when using fresh herbs. When a plant is alive, its pH

HERB SUBSTITUTIONS

INGREDIENT	SUGGESTED SUBSTITUTIONS
Basil	Oregano Thyme Parsley
Cilantro	Parsley Basil Mint
Rosemary	Thyme Savory Sage
Dill	Fennel fronds Tarragon
Parsley	Cilantro Chervil Basil
Sage	Poultry seasoning Rosemary Marjoram
Thyme	Oregano Basil Savory

value can affect the recipe's overall pH value. Dried herbs are generally more concentrated in flavor when compared to fresh herbs. The drying process removes the water content from the herbs, which intensifies their flavor. This concentration in flavor means you generally use less dried herbs in a recipe compared to fresh, with little to no impact on the recipe's overall pH value. It is why dried herbs are most favored when preserving water-bath recipes.

As a general rule of thumb, you may use about one third the amount of dried herbs when substituting them for fresh herbs. For example, if a recipe calls for 1 tablespoon of fresh herbs, you may use 1 teaspoon of dried herbs. But what do you do if you do not like the herb listed in the canning recipe? While changing the herbs and spices will alter the recipe's flavor profile, it allows you to customize the profile to suit your palate and dietary needs.

Use the list of herb and spice substitutions on page 50 to create a flavor profile similar to what was intended but without using an herb or spice you detest. You will gain confidence as you learn what works best when customizing a meal in a jar.

Keep in mind that herb and spice substitutions may affect the intended flavor profile of the recipe, so it's important to consider the overall taste and balance when making a substitution. My advice is to taste as you go. You can always add more seasonings down the road, but once they are added to the stockpot, they cannot be removed.

When Not to Substitute Vegetable Ingredients

If you do not like, or cannot eat, the main ingredient in a canning recipe, you cannot create a substitute. For instance, home-canned spaghetti sauce. Tomatoes are the main ingredient, which is the foundation for the entire recipe. If you do not like tomatoes, you cannot substitute another vegetable because it would then alter the entire recipe. In this case, you would simply not be able to create and preserve spaghetti sauce.

Another example is asparagus soup. Asparagus is the main ingredient, and choosing another vegetable to replace asparagus would change the entirety of the recipe.

VEGETABLE SUBSTITUTIONS

We all have our own personal style, likes, dislikes, and favorites. That can be said for anything, really, including food. How many times have you looked at a canning recipe and were ready to preserve it until you realized it had one or two ingredients you just couldn't stand to ingest? Or, God forbid, you have a food allergy and simply cannot partake in what the ingredient list has to offer.

While most water-bath recipes cannot be modified, the red tape is cut when using a pressure canner. For instance, when a recipe's pH is so low it requires it to be processed at a standard 10 PSI and the processing time is 90 minutes for quart

VEGETABLE SUBSTITUTIONS

INGREDIENT	SUGGESTED SUBSTITUTIONS
Onions	Shallots
	Leeks
	Scallions
Bell peppers	Cubanelle peppers
	Poblano peppers
	Anaheim peppers
	Pimiento peppers
	Banana peppers
	Bok Choy
Carrots	Parsnips
	Sweet potatoes
	Turnips
Celery	Fennel
	Bok choy
Spinach	Swiss chard
	Kale
	Beet greens
	Collard greens
	Mustard greens
	Bok choy
Green beans	Wax beans
	Snow peas
Radishes	Carrots
	Kohlrabi
	Cabbage
Asparagus	Green beans
	Snap peas
	Broccoli stalks
Beets	Turnips
	Rutabaga
Eggplant	Zucchini
	Summer squash
	Celery root

Food Allergies and Safe Canning

If you are allergic to a particular ingredient, omit it from the canning recipe without hesitation. You may use the handy Vegetable Substitution Chart to find an alternative solution, or simply increase another ingredient by the amount omitted to keep the vegetable ratio in balance.

jars and 75 minutes for pint jars, we have a bit of room to safely customize our recipe using ingredients we love.

For example, many canners fell in love with my chicken pot pie filling pressure-canning recipe. For over 10 years this recipe has been published on my website (www.canningdiva.com), giving us the ability to create and preserve a delicious low-acid, meat-based pie filling to later use in a pie, atop biscuits, or however we choose to please our family and guests. As the canning recipe grew in popularity, canners began reaching out to me to share how they did not like peas or would prefer to add green beans or potatoes. Some even wished to add dark meat but were unsure how to do so seeing as my recipe called for chicken breast meat only.

Each time I answered with the same response, and this answer resonates for recipes that process at 10 PSI or higher for 90 minutes or 75 minutes for quarts or pints, respectively:

"When you tally up the total amount of vegetables and the total amount of meat within the recipe, you learn there is a ratio between the two food groups. For chicken pot pie filling, the recipe requires 10 cups of meat to 13 cups of vegetables. As long as you stay within the recipe's ratios, you may substitute the vegetable(s) of your liking and use the cut of meat you prefer."

To break it down further, here is the list of ingredients to make and preserve chicken pot pie filling in a jar:

10 (8 oz.) bone-in, skin-on
    chicken breasts, chopped (10 cups)

4 T. butter

1 large onion, diced (2 cups)

8 celery ribs, diced (2 cups)

9 carrots, peeled and diced (5 cups)

4 cups frozen peas

1 T. salt

2 tsp. black pepper

2 tsp. celery seeds

2 tsp. garlic powder

1⅓ cups ClearJel

8 cups chicken broth

As you can see, the canner who asked if they could omit the green peas can easily do so by either replacing the green peas with 4 cups of another vegetable, like corn kernels, cut green beans, or cubed potatoes (or any combination thereof), or by omitting the peas and increasing the existing vegetables by a total of 4 cups. Regardless, the 13-cup vegetable to 10-cup meat ratio remains the same.

Another example would be if an individual wished to use their poultry on hand. In doing so, they might wind up having more dark meat available than white meat. Or maybe the individual has leftover turkey meat after a holiday feast. So long as the total yield of meat equals 10 cups chopped, the recipe can be made using any cut of poultry available.

When creating and preserving the recipes throughout this book, use this handy chart of suggested substitutions to help you customize the vegetables within each recipe to your liking.

The cool thing about the substitution chart is it works both ways. For example, if the recipe calls for shallots, and all you have on hand or enjoy eating are yellow onions, then use the yellow onions as a substitute. Or if you prefer to use 1 cup of chopped fennel rather than 1 cup of chopped celery in a recipe, you may do so, so long as the unit of measurement remains the same. Just keep in mind, when you swap out a recipe's intended ingredient for another option, you will likely change the flavor, texture, and visual appearance of the recipe.

Last, and most importantly, pressure-canning recipes that do not process at the standard PSI for the full 90 or 75 minutes cannot be modified or customized. Meaning, if a recipe only processes for 75 minutes for quarts or 55 minutes for pints at 10 PSI, the recipe must be made as written and cannot be adjusted, modified, or substituted. The reason we are able to process these recipes for a shorter period of time is because of the overall acidic value and its overall density, or thickness. To change, omit, or replace an ingredient could change the recipe's overall pH and could require a longer processing time.

OILS AND FATS

In the vast culinary world, oils and fats play a fundamental role in crafting delicious and satisfying meals. They serve as the foundation upon which flavors are built, enhancing taste, texture, and the overall culinary experience. From the sizzle of a hot pan to the artistry of home canning, oils and fats are essential components that deserve our attention and understanding.

Throughout each recipe chapter, you will notice I begin most, if not all, of my recipes with either an oil or a fat. There are a variety of oils we can use when we are creating the foundation of a recipe, and the oil is typically selected based on the specific cuisine. As you thumb through the pages you will notice Mediterranean cuisine primarily uses olive oil and will often use the fat from the meat being seared or browned. In Asian cuisine, the recipes use vegetable oil and sometimes peanut oil. Both Asian and Middle Eastern cuisines share the use of sesame oil, depending on the dish.

While there isn't a "wrong oil" per se, the importance of selecting the proper oil to obtain the true nature of the dish has been frivolously debated in the culinary world. It is why you will see such a variety throughout the book. Please know, at the end of the day, if having nine different oils in your cupboard is unachievable, you may simply use the oil you cook with at home.

Of course, using the oil you cook with is a substitution of convenience. However, I hope to expand your options and provide you with information on the differences in oils so you may make an informed choice as to which oil you will substitute.

1. **Olive Oil:** A staple in Mediterranean cuisine, olive oil offers a rich, fruity flavor and is well suited for salad dressings, sautéing, and drizzling over finished dishes.

2. **Canola Oil:** Known for its neutral flavor and high smoke point, canola oil is versatile and suitable for various cooking methods such as frying, baking, and roasting.

3. **Vegetable Oil:** A widely used and affordable option, vegetable oil is a blend of different oils and has a neutral taste. It is suitable for frying, stir-frying, and baking.

4. **Peanut Oil:** With a mild flavor and high smoke point, peanut oil is popular in Asian cuisines. It adds a distinctive taste and is commonly used for stir-frying.

5. **Sesame Oil:** Commonly found in Asian and Middle Eastern cuisines, sesame oil adds a rich, nutty aroma and flavor to dishes. It is also used as a finishing oil due to its intense flavor.

6. **Coconut Oil:** Widely used in tropical and Asian cuisines, coconut oil lends a subtle coconut flavor and aroma to dishes. It is versatile and suitable for baking, sautéing, and high-heat cooking.

7. **Avocado Oil:** Known for its high smoke point and mild flavor, avocado oil is ideal for high-heat cooking methods like grilling and roasting. It also works well in salad dressings and marinades.

8. **Grapeseed Oil:** Extracted from grape seeds, this oil has a light, neutral taste, and a high smoke point. It is suitable for sautéing, frying, and baking.

9. **Sunflower Oil:** Sunflower oil is a versatile cooking oil with a neutral taste and a high smoke point. It is commonly used for frying, baking, and salad dressings.

THE BUTTER MYTH

It's important to address the misconception that butter is considered a dairy product in the culinary context of home canning. Butter, in its pure form, is not considered a dairy product. Let's delve into the scientific explanation and clarify the minuscule levels of dairy within butter.

Butter is primarily composed of milk fat, which is derived from the cream of milk. During the process of churning cream, the fat globules present in the cream separate from the liquid portion, known as buttermilk. The remaining solid component is what we know as butter. While butter is made from milk, the final product has an extremely low level of dairy components. This is due to the churning process, which effectively removes most of the water-soluble proteins, sugars, and lactose present in milk. As a result, butter contains less than 1 percent of the lactose found in whole milk and very minimal amounts of casein and whey proteins, which are the primary components that may cause issues for individuals with dairy allergies or lactose intolerance.

In the context of home canning, it's important to emphasize butter itself is considered a low-risk food when it comes to food safety. The acidity level in butter is too low (the lower the pH means a higher acidic value) to support the growth of harmful bacteria or other microorganisms, which may cause foodborne illnesses. Further, in the culinary world, butter is the most common fat used for cooking, baking, and home canning. Depending on the cuisine, a pressure-canning recipe may incorporate all three types of fat (oil, butter, and animal fat) to bring out the best flavor profile of each ingredient.

Substitutions for Butter and Oil

People with dairy allergies or lactose intolerance should consult with healthcare professionals or registered dietitians to determine the suitability of butter for their specific dietary needs. And for those of you who are watching your saturated fat intake, it would stand to reason that butter may no longer be on your grocery list. In this case, substituting cooking oil for butter is a perfectly safe and delicious option when pressure canning a meal in a jar. Another substitute you may use in place of butter when pressure canning is ghee or clarified butter. Ghee is commonly used in Indian and South Asian cuisines and is gaining popularity in America. It has a rich, nutty flavor and a high smoke point. It is ideal for sautéing, frying, and adding richness to dishes.

Ghee is made by simmering butter to remove the milk solids and water content. It is heated until the water evaporates and the solids separate and sink to the bottom. The remaining golden liquid is clarified butter, which is then strained to remove any remaining solids. Ghee has a longer shelf life than butter and is known for its unique flavor and cooking properties. It also makes a wonderful substitution for butter and many cooking oils when cooking and home canning.

Using Coconut Milk or Cream

Another fat often used in home canning that has received undeserved angst is coconut milk. Sadly, many are misguided to believe that if an ingredient possesses the name "milk" it is therefore a dairy product. In a culinary context, the term *milk* is used to describe the consistency of an ingredient or recipe. We say things like "it has a milky, silky texture," or "that is smooth like milk." The term *milk* is a description of a liquid that has similar characteristics and features to milk, but that does not mean it is literally a dairy product like cow's milk.

Coconut milk and coconut cream are widely used as plant-based alternatives to dairy and fats in culinary contexts. They are derived from the flesh of mature coconuts and have a rich, creamy texture and a distinct coconut flavor. Coconut milk and cream provide a creamy and thick consistency to dishes in both savory and sweet recipes. Both contain a higher fat content compared to other plant-based milks.

Because coconut milk and cream have a high fat content, a recipe like curried salmon (page 108) may naturally separate after pressure canning and cooling. This separation into a solid, creamy layer and a thin watery layer does not make it unsafe for consumption; rather the separation of fat into solids is just as normal of an occurrence as when we pressure-can beef stock in a jar. The natural separation is resolved by emptying a jar into a saucepan and gently heating and stirring it before serving.

THICKENING AGENTS

If you have made some of my pressure-canning recipes, you will notice I often instruct you to hot pack your jars by first using a slotted spoon before ladling hot liquid, or broth, into the jar. This vital instruction is given so the individual has full control over the ratio of liquids to solids within each jar. It also helps prevent an inconsistency in the texture and thickness of the recipe within each jar during processing.

Take, for example, beef stew. If you were to merely ladle it into jars after it cooked on the stovetop, some jars would have more solids while the final jar will wind up with much of the remaining stew broth and limited solids. While this might not sound like a big deal at the start, after processing said quart jars at 240°F (116°C) for 90 minutes, you will certainly see why the ratios are important. As they say, we are in the thick of it.

Foods That Naturally Thicken Recipes

Beef stew is loaded with root crop vegetables, and the primary ingredient next to beef is potatoes. Potatoes are a natural thickening agent used in the culinary process to thicken soups, stews, sauces, and gravies, as well as casseroles and baked dishes. Whether on the stovetop or in the oven, each jar is essentially the same environment, and as the potato breaks down from the heat and moisture, the dish will develop a creamy texture.

There is nothing wrong with thickening a home-canning recipe—we do it all the time. However, we do so by using a controlled ratio of liquids to solids. Like in the example of beef stew, if we do not control the ratio within the jar's contained environment, we wind up with one jar being excessively thick, another jar being partially thick, and the last jar being a liquid mess with nothing but food particles floating about. Who wants to eat that last jar of "beef stew" for dinner? Not me.

When packing jars, we must control the jar's balance of solids to liquids to maximize jar space and show a consistent proportion in each jar. Further, it is imperative we properly manage the recipe's overall thickness, or density, when creating and preserving pressure-canning recipes.

When I use food to thicken a recipe, these natural thickening ingredients are carefully measured and tested to ensure the right consistency is achieved in batch after batch, time and time again. In addition to potatoes, there are a variety of ingredients used throughout this book that have been carefully selected and measured to obtain a thick texture without becoming too dense to prevent a full transfer of heat, or thermal transfer, throughout each ingredient during processing.

Here is a list of some of the foods that naturally thicken pressure-canning recipes:

- White fleshed potatoes
- Dried beans (kidney, black, chickpea, cannellini)
- Lentils
- Apples
- Dried fruits
- Coconut cream and coconut milk
- Pumpkin and squash
- Sweet potatoes
- Tomato paste

When exposed to heat for a specific period of time, each of these foods will break down and thicken the recipe. Some, like tomato paste, are so concentrated that they absorb a portion of the recipe's moisture. Others, such as lentils, are specifically chosen to create the thickened base for the recipe. It is for this reason we cannot deviate from the ingredient's measurement, or substitute a lentil for a dried bean, when pressure canning.

For example, if the recipe calls for 1 cup of lentils, you cannot add 1½ cups of lentils to the recipe. Doing so will cause the liquid in the recipe to become fully absorbed, and the center mass may become too dense in the jar. It could also cause the lentils to absorb so much moisture they swell themselves right out the jar, preventing the lid from sealing and making a horrible mess inside the pressure canner.

What we can do, however, is substitute canned beans or a similarly sized dried bean. For instance, if the recipe calls for cannellini beans and you do not have access to them, or do not enjoy eating them, you may use a navy or great northern bean instead. Additionally, if a recipe calls for green lentils, and you only have brown lentils on hand, you may safely make the swap. There will be a slight trade-off in flavor with such substitutions, but nothing unsafe in relation to food preservation.

Finally, you will see times I have included ClearJel in the list of ingredients. ClearJel is the only approved corn starch for home canning because it will not impede the heat transfer during processing. Also, it will not lose its viscosity when exposed to acidic ingredients like tomatoes, it can withstand high temperatures, and it will thicken again when reheated.

If you do not have access to ClearJel, you may safely omit it from the pressure-canning recipe and later thicken your home-canned meal on the stovetop before serving. Depending on the recipe itself and its intended flavor, you may use a dehydrated food from the list above as a substitute for ClearJel, like dried potato flakes.

SUBSTITUTIONS FOR ALCOHOL

Wine is used as a flavor enhancement to a variety of dishes. It adds depth, complexity, and richness by infusing the ingredients with unique flavors. Different types of wine produce distinct flavor profiles that complement the taste and flavor of various ingredients. Because wine is acidic and has enzymes that break down proteins, it is a wonderful way to tenderize meat used in the canning recipe.

A common term you will see throughout

The Yolk About Eggs

Fresh egg yolk is comprised of 50% water, 30% fat, and 20% protein and retains an almost neutral pH of 6.4-6.7, similar in pH to butter and oil. Further, egg yolk contains lecithin, an emulsifier making it an excellent binding agent. In this book, you will notice the use of egg yolk as a fat and binding agent when making meatballs. Because we used lean meat when making meatballs, the egg yolk provides ample fat to avoid dry meatballs and binds the ingredients together so they retain their shape. After testing the use of egg yolk as a fat and binding agent in these pressure-canning recipes, I am pleased to report its safety and impressive resolve despite the high heat, long processing times, and hermetic environment. Do note, because the pH of the albumen, the egg white, which is 63 times more alkaline than the yolk (very low acidity of 9.3-9.5 pH), only the yolk is advised suitable to create and preserve meatballs using a pressure canner.

[Stadelman, W.J. and O.J. Cotterill, ed. *Egg Science and Technology*, 4th ed. (New York: The Haworth Press, 1995), 115-119.]

the recipe chapters is an instruction to *deglaze*. Wine is often used to deglaze a pan after cooking meats or vegetables. This culinary term is used to describe the action of using a liquid to help loosen and dissolve the flavorful browned bits stuck to the bottom of the pan, which helps create the sauce used in the recipe. The wine is slowly added to the pan while you stir and scrape the browned bits from the bottom of the pan.

In every recipe that incorporates wine as an ingredient, I have given you suggestions as to which style of wine to choose based on its grape variety and the combination of the recipe's ingredients. When it comes to which brand to buy, I tell all my students to cook with what you drink or with something close to it. I also tell my students not to use cooking wine. Cooking wine has a higher alcohol flavor and is loaded with preservatives and salt which is the best way to ruin a beautifully crafted recipe. So please do not head to the baking aisle at the store when purchasing wine for canning (or cooking).

If you do not drink wine or use alcohol, you may substitute using more of the broth or stock listed in the ingredients. For example, if the recipe calls for 5 cups of beef broth and 1 cup of red wine, increase the beef broth to 6 cups. If the instructions tell you to deglaze the pan with the red wine, use an equal amount of beef broth instead and then add additional broth as instructed.

MEAT SUBSTITUTIONS

Meat substitutes, also known as plant-based meats or meat alternatives, offer a range of benefits for those individuals who do not eat meat from birds or other animals. These substitutes accommodate dietary restrictions and allergies, while still providing a protein source. With a variety of flavors and textures, they offer culinary versatility in re-creating familiar meat-based dishes.

After extensive testing, I am happy to report there are several meat substitutes suitable for pressure canning. Chapter 10, "Vegetarian Cuisine," primarily utilizes a variety of meat substitutes, however, you will see other meatless recipes peppered throughout the book.

Here is a list of meat alternatives and substitutions you may confidently use to create meatless protein-packed pressure-canning recipes:

- Soy plant-based meat
- Tofu
- Jackfruit

Soy plant-based meats, also known as soy meat alternatives or soy-based meat substitutes, are products made from soy protein isolate or textured soy protein designed to resemble the texture, appearance, and taste of traditional meat. These plant-based meats are created by processing soybeans into various forms, such as patties, crumbles, or strips, and then combining them with other ingredients to enhance their flavor and texture.

Soy plant-based meats are popular among vegetarians, vegans, and individuals seeking to reduce their meat consumption, as they offer a meat-like experience while being derived from plant sources.

As you learned about denaturing harmful microorganisms in chapter 1, the food's pH must be high enough in acid (below 4.0) to inhibit the growth of harmful microorganisms. While most microorganisms prefer to thrive in a neutral pH range of 6.5 to 7.5, foodborne pathogens prefer a slightly acidic to neutral range around 4.6 to 7.0. When pressure canning low-acid foods, we rely on time and temperature during processing to denature, or kill, the microorganisms and harmful pathogens.

Like dried beans, soy plant-based meats have a pH of 6 to 6.6, making dried beans and soy plant-based meats less acidic than animal meat. Yes, you read that right, meat and poultry are slightly acidic; however, neither are acidic enough to denature harmful pathogens all on their own, which is why meat, poultry, fish, plant-based meats, and dried beans are pressure canned to become shelf stable for long-term storage.

Tofu is another popular meat substitute that is primarily used in Asian and Indian cuisines but has also found its way into Mediterranean, American, and European cuisines inspired by vegetarian and vegan diets. Tofu, sometimes called bean curd, is derived from soybeans and is a food prepared by coagulating soy milk, which results in curds, then pressing the curds into solid white blocks of varying softness. Firm tofu is the best suited for pressure canning as it has less moisture than silken or soft tofu and is able to withstand the high temperature and lengthy processing time of pressure canning without drastically losing its shape. Tofu is high in protein and low in fat and is loaded with calcium and iron. Tofu absorbs the recipe's flavors derived from the other ingredients, making it a versatile meat substitute.

After studying soy-based tofu and testing firm tofu in a variety of applications, it has proven to be a resilient meat alternative for pressure canning low-acid recipes. Let's dive into firm tofu's acidity. Raw pork and beef have a pH range from 5.4 to 6.0 and become slightly less acidic after being exposed to heat. After pork and beef are cooked and processed in jars in a pressure canner, the acidic value of the meat lowers to a range of 5.8 to 6.2. Unlike raw pork and beef, tofu starts out uncooked with a lower pH of 5.8 to 6.2, yet when exposed to heat and pressure canned, tofu becomes slightly more acidic at 6.0.

Jackfruit is a tropical fruit that originates from the regions of Southeast Asia, including countries such as India, Bangladesh, Thailand, and Malaysia. It is a large, green, spiky fruit that can grow to impressive sizes, weighing up to 80 pounds (36 kilograms). Jackfruit is renowned for its unique texture and versatility in culinary applications. The edible parts of the fruit include the sweet, fleshy bulbs that are found within the fibrous, stringy interior. These bulbs have a mild, slightly sweet flavor that can be likened to a blend of tropical fruits such as pineapple, mango, and banana.

Jackfruit is often used as a meat substitute in vegetarian and vegan dishes due to its fibrous and meat-like texture, making it a popular ingredient in savory curries, stir-fries, sandwiches, and even plant-based "pulled pork" and sloppy joe recipes (page 207). Its versatility, tropical flavor profile, and meat-like texture have made jackfruit a sought-after ingredient for those seeking plant-based alternatives or exploring new culinary experiences.

In contrast to other meat substitutes, jackfruit is slightly more acidic, with a pH range of 4.7 to 5.5, depending on which region it is grown in and how ripe it was before it was harvested. Green bell peppers have a similar pH value, ranging from 4.6 to 5.0. With the right ingredients and sauces, jackfruit can be a delicious meat substitute in pressure-canning recipes for years to come.

Ingredient substitutions when pressure canning offer a valuable opportunity to customize and enhance your home-canned recipes. By exploring alternative ingredients and techniques, you can adapt recipes to suit dietary preferences, health considerations, and flavor preferences. Whether you're substituting herbs and vegetables, finding alternatives to sugar and salt, or exploring plant-based options, the key is to understand the characteristics and properties of different ingredients.

Having the knowledge to safely provide you and your family with ingredient substitutions empowers you to take control of your food choices, adapt recipes to your specific needs, and embrace a more personalized approach to pressure canning.

Have fun creating and preserving a plethora of meals in a jar, and embrace the art of food substitution, elevating your pressure-canning experience to masterful new heights.

The Raw Stacking Method

Skip the cooking and simmering step and learn to create easy meals in a jar using the raw stacking method. This chapter will share the math and instructions so you may create and preserve delicious, evenly proportioned meals in every jar.

BENEFITS OF USING THE RAW STACKING METHOD

For decades, home canners would boil a canning recipe, then hot pack it into each jar. This process was done primarily to blend the recipe's flavors and remove any trapped air from the food's fibers, essentially preshrinking the food prior to processing. Doing so helps us obtain a higher ratio of solids to liquid in each jar. Otherwise, foods with a high water content, like tomatoes and onions, will expel liquid, causing the recipe to have more liquid than solids.

We often see this when we raw pack tomatoes. It is why you may often see two inches of liquid at the base of a jar with all the solids suspended above. Conversely, ingredients such as beans will absorb the liquid in the jar, so precooking them will aide in balancing the water absorption. Hot packing ensures every jar yields an ample amount of the recipe.

Take, for instance, beef stew. I will brown my stew meat, use wine to deglaze my pan, then add my aromatics and seasonings to create the base flavor profile, and complete the recipe by adding the stock, beef, and vegetables. I then bring everything to a boil and allow the stew to simmer for 10 minutes before filling my jars. Doing this creates a well-balanced flavor profile so when I ladle the stew into jars, I know each jar will taste the same and yield a similar ratio of solid to liquid.

This time-honored method of hot packing has been a mainstay in home canning, but it comes with a large time investment. Creating the stew from scratch, including its ingredient prep work, is a minimum two-hour time investment. Couple that with an additional two hours (or more) spent in processing the stew in a pressure canner (including the canner's time to heat up and cool down), and I'm looking at a total of four to six hours to create and preserve the beef stew. While some of us may have no issue whatsoever investing 5 hours into a single batch, other canners need a quicker way to preserve their favorite meals.

To accommodate today's busy lifestyles, canners may create an assembly-line production in their kitchen using the raw stacking method of jar packing. Often, raw stacking doesn't even require the use of the stove to cook or heat ingredients. The goal when using the raw stacking method is to properly clean and prep the food, then pack it raw into jars. When creating and testing recipes, I take into account (1) the best way to blend flavors, (2) the volume within the jar, and (3) proportionate math to duplicate the same result jar after jar.

THE RAW STACKING METHOD EXPLAINED

So how is the raw stacking method safely and effectively accomplished? The key is to consider each individual jar as the proverbial stockpot and create a ratio of solids, seasonings, and liquid to yield a positive, safe, and delicious result. The process of raw stacking is essentially raw packing the ingredients but doing so using premeasured amounts and layering them onto one another.

The placement of each layer is well-thought-out to yield a desirable result and protect the integrity of each ingredient. For example, dried beans should never be stacked next to an acid like tomatoes. Doing so will prevent the beans from softening during processing. As a recipe creator, I also take into account the amount of liquid each raw ingredient will expel or absorb to determine how it will react in the jar alongside other ingredients once everything is exposed to heat.

Let's re-create the beef stew recipe using the raw stacking method (see recipe, page 69). For starters, browning the meat is now only a personal preference; it is no longer a requirement. Second, the liquid used becomes your flavor profile and is treated like we would a pickling brine, meaning we combine the liquids and seasonings together, bring the mixture to a boil, and then simmer the liquid to infuse it with the seasonings.

After adding a bay leaf and thyme sprig to each jar, the beef stew meat is added making it the base layer. Premeasured amounts of potato, carrot, tomato, and onion are added one layer at a time. It is vital to compress, or push down, each layered ingredient after it is added. We need to pack each jar full of raw ingredients first before adding any liquid. Sometimes, we will fill each jar to the required headspace of solids and add liquid just to fill in the spaces that remain. At other times, the solids will fill only three-quarters of the jar, with liquid filling the remaining top quarter. It depends on the recipe. Essentially, each jar is its very own "stockpot" of beef stew ready for processing.

After processing, the ingredients often remain in their respective layers but are now fully cooked. You will notice shrinkage of some ingredients and swelling of others. You will also notice the liquid is reminiscent of soup rather than stew, just as it appears when you ladle it into each jar.

The speed and simplicity of raw stacking can help us put up as many jars as possible during canning season. In the case of raw stacking beef stew however, it will not produce the thick, hearty texture we usually see in a stockpot. While each jar is a well-balanced version of its predecessor, its consistency is thinner and more soup-like. The good news is that there is still a way we may achieve a stew-like appearance when we open a jar to heat it on the stovetop prior to serving. Just invest a little time into thickening the stew on the stovetop with a flour and water slurry prior to serving. Or incorporate the raw stacked beef stew into another meal creation like a potpie filling or open-faced beef sandwiches.

CANNING RECIPES NOT SUITED FOR RAW STACKING

While the raw stacking method is a time-saver for us canners, it sadly does not apply to nor have a positive result for every canning recipe. What must be considered is the food's overall integrity and recipe's flavor. For instance, trying to replicate the delicate balance of flavors achieved when making spaghetti sauce is virtually impossible using the raw stacking method. The amount of work we would have to put into the recipe after opening a jar outweighs the time-saving benefits during the canning process. So, in this case, it is best to create the spaghetti sauce in the traditional manner and then preserve it in jars.

Another example of what not to raw stack would be chicken pot pie filling or beef burgundy. Achieving the desired texture and robust flavor profile requires too many steps to convert either recipe into a raw stacking recipe. There is value in putting time and effort in up front to produce a delicious result.

The recipes in this chapter will help you gain experience using the raw stacking method. You will soon see its many benefits and learn how to decipher which recipes the method serves best. Have fun creating and preserving these deliciously simple recipes to enjoy year after year.

Tips for Easy Raw Stacking

1. Use wide-mouthed jars. It makes raw stacking easier when packing each ingredient layer. Regular-mouthed jars will work, however, mouth space is limited for insertion and packing.

2. If you're preserving cold ingredients with a hot liquid, keep the jars warm in the dishwasher or kitchen sink prior to packing. Rest the jars on a cutting board when packing and filling with hot liquid.

3. To save time, wash, prep, and cut your ingredients the day before and store them in the refrigerator. When you're ready to pack the jars, create an assembly line with your ingredients to speed the packing process.

4. Use a headspace-measuring tool or wooden spoon to press each raw ingredient layer down after adding it to the jar. Maximizing space is essential to keep a good ratio of solids to liquid.

5. When adding crushed or powdered dried seasonings to each jar, add them as the last ingredient before the liquid so they are at the top of the jar. When you slowly ladle liquid into each jar, the dried seasonings will disperse throughout the jar, creating a robust flavor profile.

6. To release the trapped air pockets that will form once you fill the jars with liquid, press down onto the ingredients with your headspace tool and gently tap the jar onto a cutting board to break the air pockets loose. Add additional liquid to maintain the headspace if necessary.

Beef Stew

Hearty beef stew is a well-known comfort food, especially for those who must weather winter temperatures for months on end. Serve this delicious meal in a jar alongside freshly baked bread or thicken and serve atop mashed potatoes.

PREP TIME: 30 minutes **COOK TIME:** 5 minutes
PROCESS TIME: 90 or 75 minutes **YIELD:** 7 quarts or 14 pints

DIRECTIONS

1. Place the beef stock, wine, Worcestershire sauce, oregano, basil, salt, and black pepper in a stockpot and bring it to a boil over medium-high heat. Mix well. Reduce the heat and simmer the stock mixture for 5 minutes, then remove from heat.

2. Add a bay leaf and a sprig of thyme to each quart jar. For each quart jar, add the following ingredients in layers, pressing down each ingredient before adding the next. If canning in pints, halve the amount of each ingredient, including the bay leaf and thyme sprig. Pack the jars up to a 1-inch headspace.

   a. **1½ cups beef stew meat**

   b. **½ cup potatoes**

   c. **½ cup carrots**

   d. **¼ cup tomatoes**

   e. **2 T. onion**

3. Ladle the warm stock mixture into each jar, leaving 1 inch of headspace. Press and gently tap the jar bottom on a cutting board to remove any trapped air pockets. Add additional stock if necessary to maintain the 1-inch headspace.

4. Wipe the jar rims with a washcloth dipped in vinegar. Place the lid and ring on each jar and hand tighten.

5. Process in a pressure canner at 10 PSI or according to your elevation and canner type. Process quart jars for 90 minutes and pint jars for 75 minutes.

INGREDIENTS

5 cups beef stock

1 cup red wine (or substitute with stock or water)

2 T. Worcestershire sauce

1 T. dried oregano

1 T. dried basil

1 tsp. salt (optional)

½ tsp. ground black pepper

7 bay leaves

7 sprigs fresh thyme

7 lbs. beef stew meat, cut into 1½-inch pieces (10½ cups)

4 cups potatoes, peeled and cut into 1-inch pieces

4 cups carrots, peeled and cut into 1-inch pieces

2 cups tomatoes, diced

1 cup onion, diced

Meat and Vegetable Varieties

INGREDIENTS

Amount per Quart Jar

1 cup ground meat, seasoned and browned

1 cup vegetable

1 cup starch

2 T. onion

1 T. seasoning (fresh or dried)

2 cups liquid (water, stock, or broth)

INGREDIENT TIP:

For pint jars, simply cut the measurements in half.

PREP TIME: 30 minutes   **COOK TIME:** None

PROCESS TIME: 90 or 75 minutes   **YIELD:** 6 quarts or 12 pints

Use these four fun recipes to achieve the flavor combination your family will love. Get creative! Using the tested ratios of protein to vegetables, each jar will provide the perfect meal on the go.

DIRECTIONS

1. Add each ingredient in order, raw stacking in layers, pressing down each ingredient before adding the next. Fill each jar to a generous 1¼-inch headspace.

2. Wipe the jar rims with a washcloth dipped in vinegar. Place the lid and ring on each jar and hand tighten.

3. Process in a pressure canner at 10 PSI or according to your elevation and canner type. Process quart jars for 90 minutes and pint jars for 75 minutes.

VARIATIONS

Ground Chicken

3 lbs. ground chicken, seasoned and browned (6 cups)

6 cups green beans (fresh or frozen), cut into 1-inch pieces

6 medium yellow potatoes, scrubbed and chopped (6 cups)

6 green onions, diced (¾ cup)

Oregano or rosemary (or other herbs, to taste)

12 cups chicken stock

Ground Beef

3 lbs. ground beef, seasoned and browned (6 cups)

6 cups green peas (fresh or frozen)

6 medium red skin potatoes, scrubbed and chopped (6 cups)

1 small red onion, diced (¾ cup)

Minced garlic (optional, to taste)

12 cups beef stock

Ground Turkey

3 lbs. ground turkey, seasoned and browned (6 cups)

3 large sweet potatoes, peeled and chopped (6 cups)

1 head cabbage, chopped (6 cups)

1 small sweet onion, diced (¾ cup)

Parsley (optional, to taste)

12 cups chicken stock

Ground Pork

3 lbs. ground pork, seasoned and browned (6 cups)

2 bok choy, chopped (6 cups)

3 turnips, scrubbed and chopped (6 cups)

6 green onions, diced (¾ cup)

Fennel seeds (optional, to taste)

12 cups chicken stock

Ham and Kale Soup

Enjoy the smoky flavor of ham in this power-packed soup recipe. Using fresh kale and great northern beans, create a sustaining meal in a jar in minutes. When you're ready to eat it, simply heat a jar on the stovetop and top with Parmesan cheese before serving.

PREP TIME: 30 minutes   COOK TIME: 0 minutes
PROCESS TIME: 90 or 75 minutes   YIELD: 7 quarts or 14 pints

DIRECTIONS

1. Thoroughly rinse the dried beans in a colander, being sure to remove any rocks, debris, or disfigured beans. Place the beans in a stockpot and cover them with water. Using your hands, agitate the beans in the water to remove any dirt. Empty the beans into the colander and rinse them again.

2. For each quart jar, add the following ingredients in layers, pressing down each ingredient before adding the next. If canning in pints, halve the amount of each ingredient.

   a. **¼ cup beans**
   b. **1 cup ham**
   c. **1 cup kale**
   d. **½ cup carrots**
   e. **¼ cup onion**
   f. **¼ cup celery**
   g. **1 tsp. garlic**

3. Pour the broth into each jar, leaving 1 inch of headspace. Press and gently tap the jar bottom on cutting board to remove any trapped air pockets. Add additional broth if necessary to maintain the 1-inch headspace.

4. Wipe the jar rims with a washcloth dipped in vinegar. Place the lid and ring on each jar and hand tighten.

5. Process in a pressure canner at 10 PSI or according to your elevation and canner type. Process quart jars for 90 minutes and pint jars for 75 minutes.

INGREDIENTS

2 cups dried navy or great northern beans

2½ lbs. smoked ham steak, diced into ½-inch cubes (7 cups)

2 bunches kale, stems removed and chopped (7 cups)

4 cups carrots, peeled and cut into 1-inch pieces

2 cups onion, diced

2 cups celery, diced

7 tsp. minced garlic

14 cups chicken or vegetable broth

Hearty Chicken Soup

This hearty soup is filled with plenty of vegetables and protein to give you a sustainable meal no matter the time of day. Using elements from traditional chicken soup, the flavor and nutrients abound. Feel free to add a dash of salt and pepper when heating the soup to serve.

PREP TIME: 20 minutes   COOK TIME: 0 minutes
PROCESS TIME: 90 or 75 minutes   YIELD: 7 quarts or 14 pints

INGREDIENTS

3½ cups dried navy or great northern beans

7 small boneless, skinless chicken breasts, cut into 2-inch pieces (7 cups)

4 cups carrots, peeled and cut into 1-inch pieces

1 cup onion, diced

1 cup celery, diced

7 tsp. minced garlic

7 bay leaves

14 cups chicken stock

4 cups water

DIRECTIONS

1. Thoroughly rinse the dried beans in a colander, being sure to remove any rocks, debris, or disfigured beans. Place the beans in a stockpot and cover them with water. Using your hands, agitate the beans in the water to remove any dirt. Empty the beans into the colander and rinse them again.

2. For each quart jar, add the following ingredients in layers, pressing down each ingredient before adding the next. If canning in pints, halve the amount of each ingredient.

   a. **½ cup beans**
   b. **1 cup chicken**
   c. **½ cup carrot**
   d. **2 T. onion**
   e. **2 T. celery**
   f. **1 tsp. garlic**
   g. **1 bay leaf**

3. Add the chicken stock and water to a large pot and mix them together. Ladle the stock mixture into each jar, leaving a 1-inch headspace. Gently tap the jar bottom on a cutting board to remove any trapped air pockets. Add additional broth if necessary to maintain the 1-inch headspace.

4. Wipe the jar rims with a washcloth dipped in vinegar. Place the lid and ring on each jar and hand tighten.

5. Process in a pressure canner at 10 PSI or according to your elevation and canner type. Process quart jars for 90 minutes and pint jars for 75 minutes.

Easy Vegetable Stew

Such a simple way to get all your veggies in one jar! Create this delicious soup using either fresh or frozen vegetables. For added flavor, feel free to incorporate a fresh herb or dried seasoning of your choice to each jar.

PREP TIME: 30 minutes   **COOK TIME:** 0 minutes
PROCESS TIME: 85 or 55 minutes   **YIELD:** 7 quarts or 14 pints

DIRECTIONS

1. Thoroughly rinse the dried beans in a colander, being sure to remove any rocks, debris, or disfigured beans. Place the beans in a stockpot and cover them with water. Using your hands, agitate the beans in the water to remove any dirt. Empty the beans into the colander and rinse them again.

2. For each quart jar, add the following ingredients in layers, pressing down each ingredient before adding the next. If canning in pints, halve the amount of each ingredient.

   a. **½ cup dried beans**
   b. **½ cup carrots**
   c. **½ cup green beans**
   d. **½ cup tomatoes**
   e. **½ cup green peas**
   f. **½ cup corn**
   g. **¼ cup onion**
   h. **¼ cup celery**
   i. **1 tsp. minced garlic**

3. Pour the vegetable broth into each jar, leaving 1 inch of headspace. Press and gently tap the jar bottom on a cutting board to remove any trapped air pockets. Add additional broth if necessary to maintain the 1-inch headspace.

4. Wipe the jar rims with a washcloth dipped in vinegar. Place the lid and ring on each jar and hand tighten.

5. Process in a pressure canner at 10 PSI or according to your elevation and canner type. Process quart jars for 85 minutes and pint jars for 55 minutes.

INGREDIENTS

3½ cups dried lima beans

4 cups carrots, peeled and cut into 1-inch pieces

4 cups green beans (fresh or frozen), cut into 1-inch pieces

4 cups tomatoes, diced

4 cups green peas (fresh or frozen), cut into 1-inch pieces

4 cups corn kernels (fresh or frozen)

2 cups onion, diced

2 cups celery, diced

7 tsp. minced garlic

14 cups vegetable broth

Irish Bean and Cabbage Stew

The cabbage and beans make this a stick-to-the-ribs meal in each jar. The sweetness of the carrots and sweet potatoes offset the earthy flavor of the beans and cabbage. I will often heat up a pint on the stovetop for lunch and crush a few soda crackers on top.

PREP TIME: 25 minutes **COOK TIME:** 0 minutes
PROCESS TIME: 90 or 75 minutes **YIELD:** 6 quarts or 12 pints

INGREDIENTS

3 cups dried pinto beans

3 cups onion, diced

4 celery ribs, finely chopped (¾ cup)

¼ cup minced garlic

3 medium sweet potatoes, peeled and cubed (3 cups)

10 medium carrots, peeled and diced (3 cups)

½ head green cabbage, chopped (3 cups)

10 cups beef broth

DIRECTIONS

1. Thoroughly rinse the dried beans in a colander, being sure to remove any rocks, debris, or disfigured beans. Place the beans in a stockpot and cover them with water. Using your hands, agitate the beans in the water to remove any dirt. Empty the beans into the colander and rinse them again.

2. For each quart jar, add the following ingredients in layers, pressing down each ingredient before adding the next. If canning in pints, halve the amount of each ingredient. Pack jars to 1-inch headspace.

   a. ½ cup beans
   b. ½ cup loosely packed onion
   c. 2 T. celery
   d. 2 tsp. garlic
   e. ½ cup sweet potato
   f. ½ cup carrots
   g. ½ cup loosely packed cabbage

3. Pour the beef broth into each jar leaving 1 inch of headspace. Press and gently tap the jar bottom on a cutting board to remove any trapped air pockets. Add additional broth if necessary to maintain the 1-inch headspace.

4. Wipe the jar rims with a washcloth dipped in vinegar. Place the lid and ring on each jar and hand tighten.

5. Process in a pressure canner at 10 PSI or according to your elevation and canner type. Process quart jars for 90 minutes and pint jars for 75 minutes.

Pork Fajitas

This recipe is a staple in my home. I will often substitute beef or chicken for pork to give my family options at mealtime. The authentic flavors combined with pinto beans and peppers creates a delicious combination.

PREP TIME: 30 minutes   **COOK TIME:** 0 minutes
PROCESS TIME: 90 or 75 minutes   **YIELD:** 5 quarts or 10 pints

INGREDIENTS

5 cups dried pinto beans

2 bell peppers, any color, sliced (2½ cups)

1 sweet onion, sliced (2½ cups)

5 Roma tomatoes, diced

5 lbs. pork loin, cut into strips

5 T. fajita spice blend (see below)

8 cups chicken broth

INGREDIENT TIP:

Mix the following spices to create homemade fajita seasoning:

6 T. chili powder

3 T. ground cumin

2 T. brown sugar

2 T. smoked paprika

2 T. garlic powder

2 tsp. ground mustard

2 tsp. sea salt

1 to 3 tsp. cayenne pepper

1 tsp. red pepper flakes

1 tsp. ground black pepper

DIRECTIONS

1. Thoroughly rinse the dried beans in a colander, being sure to remove any rocks, debris, or disfigured beans. Place the beans in a stockpot and cover them with water. Using your hands, agitate the beans in the water to remove any dirt. Empty the beans into the colander and rinse them again.

2. For each quart jar, add the following ingredients in layers, pressing down each ingredient before adding the next. If canning in pints, halve the amount of each ingredient. Pack jars to 1-inch headspace.

   a. **1 cup dried beans**
   b. **½ cup peppers**
   c. **½ cup onion**
   d. **1 diced tomato**
   e. **1 lb. pork loin strips (1 cup)**
   f. **1 T. fajita seasoning**

3. Pour the chicken broth into each jar leaving 1 inch of headspace. Press and gently tap the jar bottom on a cutting board to remove any trapped air pockets. Add additional broth if necessary to maintain the 1-inch headspace.

4. Wipe the jar rims with a washcloth dipped in vinegar. Place the lid and ring on each jar and hand tighten.

5. Process in a pressure canner at 10 PSI or according to your elevation and canner type. Process quart jars for 90 minutes and pint jars for 75 minutes.

Irish Shepherd's Pie in a Jar

Enjoy everything you love about traditional Irish shepherd's pie in this fun spin on a classic. Not a fan of lamb? Not to worry. Create and preserve cottage pie using ground beef. When you're ready to eat it, simply heat a jar in a saucepan, cover with your favorite shredded cheese, add a dash of salt and pepper, and serve hot!

PREP TIME: 25 minutes   COOK TIME: 10 minutes
PROCESS TIME: 90 or 75 minutes   YIELD: 6 quarts or 12 pints

DIRECTIONS

1. Place the ground lamb, onion, minced garlic, parsley, rosemary, thyme, salt (if using), and pepper in a large skillet and cook them over medium-high heat for about 8 to 10 minutes or until the meat is browned and the onion is translucent.

2. For each quart jar, add the following ingredients in layers, pressing down each ingredient before adding the next. If canning in pints, halve the amount of each ingredient. Pack jars to 1-inch headspace.

   a. **1½ cups seasoned browned lamb**
   b. **½ cup peas**
   c. **½ cup carrots**
   d. **½ cup corn kernels**
   e. **½ cup potatoes**

3. In a bowl, whisk together the beef broth, water, tomato paste, and Worcestershire sauce. Pour the broth mixture into each jar, leaving 1 inch of headspace. Press and gently tap the jar bottom on a cutting board to remove any trapped air pockets. Add additional broth if necessary to maintain the 1-inch headspace.

4. Wipe the jar rims with a washcloth dipped in vinegar. Place the lid and ring on each jar and hand tighten.

5. Process in a pressure canner at 10 PSI or according to your elevation and canner type. Process quart jars for 90 minutes and pint jars for 75 minutes.

INGREDIENTS

3 lbs. ground lamb (9 cups)

2 cups onion, chopped

2 T. minced garlic

1 T. dried parsley

2 tsp. crushed rosemary

1 tsp. dried thyme

1 tsp. salt (optional)

½ tsp. black pepper

3 cups peas (fresh or frozen)

3 cups diced carrots (fresh or frozen)

3 cups corn kernels (fresh or frozen)

3 medium potatoes, peeled and finely chopped (3 cups)

6 cups beef broth

6 cups water

1 (6 oz.) can tomato paste

2 T. Worcestershire sauce

Pepper Steak

Skip ordering takeout! Enjoy all the traditional flavors of peppered beef with this simple meal in a jar. Trust me, you will savor every bite and find yourself preserving a batch or two several times a year. Feel free to thicken the sauce with cornstarch or simply heat the meal and serve it atop a bed of jasmine rice.

PREP TIME: 40 minutes   COOK TIME: 0 minutes
PROCESS TIME: 90 or 75 minutes   YIELD: 5 quarts or 10 pints

INGREDIENTS

½ cup rice vinegar

½ cup apple cider vinegar

3½ lbs. top round roast or flank steak, thinly sliced (10 cups)

4 cups beef broth

2 cups water

1½ cups soy sauce

2 T. sriracha sauce (optional)

5 green bell peppers, cored and sliced (5 cups)

3 bunches green onions, diced (2½ cups)

5 T. minced garlic

5-inch gingerroot, peeled and minced (5 T.)

DIRECTIONS

1. Place the rice vinegar and apple cider vinegar in a glass bowl and whisk them together. Add the beef strips and toss to thoroughly coat them in the vinegar. Cover the bowl with plastic wrap and set it aside.

2. Add the beef broth, water, soy sauce, and sriracha to a large mixing bowl and whisk together. Set aside.

3. For each quart jar, add the following ingredients in layers, pressing down each ingredient before adding the next. If canning in pints, halve the amount of each ingredient.

   a. **2 cups beef**
   b. **1 cup green pepper**
   c. **½ cup green onion**
   d. **1 T. garlic**
   e. **1 T. gingerroot**

4. Give the sauce a quick whisk and pour it into each jar, leaving a generous 1¼-inch headspace. Use your headspace-measuring tool to remove any trapped air pockets. Add additional sauce if necessary to maintain the generous 1¼-inch headspace.

5. Wipe the jar rims with a washcloth dipped in vinegar. Place the lid and ring on each jar and hand tighten.

6. Process in a pressure canner at 10 PSI or according to your elevation and canner type. Process quart jars for 90 minutes and pint jars for 75 minutes.

INGREDIENT TIP: *When cutting your beef into thin strips, be sure to cut against the grain to make the meat more tender.*

5

Mediterranean Cuisine

Mediterranean cuisine is primarily made up of plants and vegetables, legumes and aromatic herbs like basil, bay leaf, chive, and fennel. Fresh fish and lean meat also complement this healthy cuisine. However, Mediterranean cuisine is not dominated by any one culture; it is influenced by a cultural exchange over periods of time throughout history.

Civilizations who bordered the Mediterranean Sea reaped the many benefits of its rich soil and perfect temperature, growing a variety of agriculture such as olives and grapes for wine. Because of its location along the sea, this region is the perfect geographical location for trading, which is how many new ingredients and spices were introduced, bolstering the region's culinary depth.

This chapter embodies the flavors and favorites from countries such as southern Spain, Italy, Greece, France, and Morocco. The use of aromatic herbs abounds within these recipes, perfect for those who grow fresh herbs year-round or simply enjoy using fresh herbs when cooking and canning. You will also notice the use of fresh seafood and chorizo sausage and pancetta, which is a staple in many recipes along the Mediterranean Sea.

Last, I have taken the liberty to include substitutions for several authentic ingredients and have given additional instructions using a variety of recipe and ingredient tips. It is my hope you'll enjoy the recipe's intended flavor profile and find options for ingredients that are readily available in your area and to your palette's liking.

Authentic Ragu Bolognese Sauce

This authentic sauce is the foundation for many classic dishes like lasagna and baked ziti and pairs beautifully with tagliatelle or fettuccine pasta. Unlike spaghetti sauce, Bolognese is made with aromatic vegetables, pancetta, and beef, which is cooked slowly in tomato sauce with a bit of stock and white wine. This recipe requires ample slow-cooking time to yield the proper consistency and is well worth the time investment.

PREP TIME: 30 minutes   COOK TIME: 90 minutes
PROCESS TIME: 90 or 75 minutes   YIELD: 5 quarts or 10 pints

INGREDIENTS

1 T. olive oil

6 medium carrots, peeled and diced (3 cups)

3 medium onions, diced (3 cups)

5 celery ribs, diced (1½ cups)

1½ lbs. pancetta, finely diced

4 lbs. 80/20 ground beef

1 cup dry white wine

6 cups tomato puree or passata

2 cups chicken stock

DIRECTIONS

1. Place the oil, carrots, onions, and celery in a stockpot and sauté the vegetables over medium heat for 8 to 10 minutes or until they have softened and the onion is translucent.

2. Add the pancetta to the stockpot and cook it for an additional 5 minutes. Add the ground beef and wine. Mix well and cook the beef for about 15 minutes or until it is browned.

3. Add the tomato puree and chicken stock to the stockpot and mix well. Bring it to a boil over medium-high heat, then reduce the heat and simmer the sauce mixture for 1 hour, stirring often to avoid scorching.

4. Using a funnel, ladle the hot Bolognese sauce into each jar, leaving 1 inch of headspace. Remove any trapped air pockets and add additional sauce if necessary to maintain the 1-inch headspace.

5. Wipe the jar rims with a washcloth dipped in vinegar. Place the lid and ring on each jar and hand tighten.

6. Process in a pressure canner at 10 PSI or according to your elevation and canner type. Process quart jars for 90 minutes and pint jars for 75 minutes.

RECIPE TIP: *When you're ready to heat and serve this recipe, empty the ragu into a saucepan and bring it to a gentle boil over medium-high heat. Add ½ cup of full fat milk for each quart jar of sauce and ¼ cup for each pint jar. Mix well, reduce the heat, and simmer the sauce for 30 minutes, then toss cooked pasta with the sauce and serve.*

French Cassoulet

Back in time, cassoulet was referred to as a peasant dish. However, this hearty mix of protein is fit for a king. When ready to eat, simply empty into oven-safe bowls, top with breadcrumbs, and bake the cassoulet in the oven at 400°F (204°C) for 10 minutes or until the top is crispy.

PREP TIME: 30 minutes   COOK TIME: 90 minutes
PROCESS TIME: 90 minutes   YIELD: 7 quarts

DIRECTIONS

1. Thoroughly rinse the beans in a colander, being sure to remove any rocks, debris, or disfigured beans. Place the beans in a stockpot and cover them with water. Bring it to a boil over high heat and allow the beans to boil for 10 minutes. Remove from heat, cover the stockpot, and steep the beans for 1 hour.

2. Heat the oil in a deep skillet over medium-high heat. Sprinkle the chicken with black pepper. Working in batches, add the chicken to the stockpot and brown each side for about 2 minutes, being careful not to overcrowd the stockpot. Using tongs, place two thighs or three legs in each quart jar and set the jars aside on cutting board.

3. Place the onion, carrots, celery, garlic, and salt pork in a separate stockpot and cook them over medium-high heat for about 8 minutes or until the onion is translucent and the pork has rendered. Add the thyme, bay leaves, pork shoulder, sausage, and chicken stock. Bring it to a boil, then reduce the heat and simmer for 15 minutes. Remove the bay leaves and discard. Remove the thyme sprigs, strip the leaves and place them into the stockpot. Discard the stems.

4. Empty the beans into a colander in the sink and quickly rinse them. Add one cup of beans to each quart jar.

5. Using a funnel and slotted spoon, evenly distribute the meat and vegetables into each jar. Ladle remaining stock into each jar leaving 1 inch of headspace. Remove any trapped air pockets and add additional stock to maintain the 1-inch headspace.

6. Wipe the jar rims with a washcloth dipped in vinegar. Place the lid and ring on each jar and hand tighten.

7. Process in a pressure canner at 10 PSI or according to your elevation and canner type. Process quart jars for 90 minutes.

INGREDIENTS

1 lb. dried cannellini beans (about 2 cups) or 4 (15 oz.) cans cannellini beans

3 T. olive oil

14 bone-in, skin-on chicken thighs (or 21 skin-on chicken or duck legs)

½ tsp. black pepper

1 large onion, diced (1½ cups)

3 medium carrots, diced (1½ cups)

2 celery ribs, diced (½ cup)

1 head garlic, peeled and minced (3 T.)

1 lb. salt pork, cut into ½-inch cubes (2½ cups)

4 sprigs thyme

2 bay leaves

1 lb. pork shoulder, cut into 1-inch cubes

1 lb. garlic sausage, sliced into ½-inch thick rounds

14 cups chicken stock

Bouillabaisse (Classic French Seafood Stew)

This delicious soup, derived from Marseille in southern France, is loaded with seafood and fresh herbs and is seasoned with saffron. Made using a variety of fish such as sea bass, haddock, halibut, and cod, it was traditionally made with whatever the fisherman hadn't sold that day. This modified version of a classic is a welcome addition to your pantry. Serve this meal hot, ladled over a slice of crusty bread adorned with rouille.

PREP TIME: 20 minutes **COOK TIME: 45 minutes**
PROCESS TIME: 160 or 100 minutes **YIELD: 5 quarts or 10 pints**

DIRECTIONS

1. Place the oil, onions, leeks, fennel, and garlic in a large stockpot and cook it over medium-high heat for about 15 minutes or until the ingredients are softened. Add the tomatoes, thyme, bay leaves, saffron, and orange zest, mix well, and cook the mixture for 1 additional minute. Slowly add the fish stock, water, and clam juice, stirring to blend the flavors. Bring it to a boil, then reduce the heat and simmer the soup for 30 minutes. Remove and discard the thyme, bay leaves, and orange zest.

2. Evenly distribute the fresh fish, clams, and squid or crab into each jar. Using a funnel, ladle the hot broth into each jar, leaving a generous 1¼-inch headspace. Remove any trapped air pockets and add additional soup if necessary to maintain the desired headspace.

3. Wipe the jar rims with a washcloth dipped in vinegar. Place the lid and ring on each jar and hand tighten.

4. Process in a pressure canner at 10 PSI or according to your elevation and canner type. Process quart jars for 160 minutes and pint jars for 100 minutes.

INGREDIENTS

3 T. olive oil

2 medium onions, diced (2 cups)

2 medium leeks, chopped (2 cups)

½ fennel bulb, thinly sliced (1 cup) or 2 tsp. fennel seeds

8 garlic cloves, minced

9 Roma tomatoes, diced (3 cups)

6 sprigs fresh thyme

3 bay leaves

1 tsp. saffron threads or ½ tsp. saffron powder

1 (3-inch) strip orange zest

4 cups fish stock

4 cups water

1 cup clam juice

4 lbs. of three different fish filets, cut into 2-inch pieces

2 lbs. clams

1 lb. squid or crab

Gigantes Plaki (Greek Butter Beans)

A great part of the Mediterranean diet relies on vegetables and legumes. Butter beans, also referred to as lima beans, are a traditional Greek side dish used to accompany meals or enjoyed as a light lunch. Its hearty and comforting nature makes this meal a delight no matter what time of day. Sprinkle the beans with chopped parsley and mint and serve them hot.

PREP TIME: 20 minutes   **COOK TIME:** 85 minutes
PROCESS TIME: 90 or 75 minutes   **YIELD:** 7 quarts or 14 pints

DIRECTIONS

1. Thoroughly rinse the dried beans in a colander, being sure to remove any rocks, debris, or disfigured beans. Place the beans in a stockpot and cover them with water. Bring it to a boil over high heat, and allow the beans to boil for 10 minutes. Remove from heat, cover the stockpot, and steep the beans for 1 hour.

2. Place the oil, onions, and garlic in a large stockpot and cook them over medium-high heat for about 10 minutes or until the onion is translucent. Add the tomatoes, tomato paste, sugar, oregano, paprika, cinnamon, and water. Mix well. Bring it to a boil, then reduce the heat and simmer the mixture, for 5 minutes.

3. Empty the steeped beans into a colander in the sink and quickly rinse them. Add 1 cup of beans to each quart jar or ½ cup of beans to each pint jar.

4. Using a funnel, ladle the tomato mixture into each jar, leaving 1 inch of headspace. Remove any trapped air pockets and add additional tomato mixture to maintain the 1-inch headspace.

5. Wipe the jar rims with a washcloth dipped in vinegar. Place the lid and ring on each jar and hand tighten.

6. Process in a pressure canner at 10 PSI or according to your elevation and canner type. Process quart jars for 90 minutes and pint jars for 75 minutes.

INGREDIENTS

4 lbs. dried butter/lima beans

3 T. olive oil

2 yellow onions, finely chopped (4 cups)

1 head garlic, peeled and minced

8 lbs. tomatoes, peeled and chopped (18 cups)

1 (6 oz.) can tomato paste

1 T. granulated sugar

1 T. dried oregano

1 T. paprika

1 T. ground cinnamon

3½ cups water

Greek Chicken and Peas

This simple meal is comprised of chicken, tomatoes, and peas and is flavored with white wine and dill weed. Enjoy this hearty dish with a piece of crusty bread to sop up its juices and a chilled glass of Greek savatiano wine.

PREP TIME: 30 minutes   COOK TIME: 13 minutes
PROCESS TIME: 90 or 75 minutes   YIELD: 7 quarts or 14 pints

INGREDIENTS

3 T. olive oil

1 large red onion, diced (3 cups)

1 cup white wine (pinot grigio or chardonnay)

4 cups vegetable or chicken broth

4 lbs. tomatoes, peeled and diced (9 cups)

2 lbs. peas (fresh or frozen)

¼ cup fresh dill, chopped or 3 T. dried dill weed

5½ lbs. boneless, skinless chicken breasts

3½ lbs. boneless, skinless chicken thighs

DIRECTIONS

1. Combine the oil and red onion in a large stockpot. Cook the onion over medium-high heat for about 8 minutes or until they are soft. Add the wine and bring it to a boil. Add the broth, tomatoes, peas, and dill. Stir well and return the tomato mixture to a boil. Reduce the heat and simmer the ingredients for 5 minutes, stirring often.

2. Place 12 ounces of chicken breasts and 8 ounces of chicken thighs into each warm quart jar or 6 ounces of chicken breasts and 4 ounces of chicken thighs into each warm pint jar. Each jar should be filled about half full. Using a funnel, ladle the tomato mixture into each jar, leaving 1 inch of headspace. Remove any trapped air pockets and add additional mixture to maintain the 1-inch headspace.

3. Wipe the jar rims with a washcloth dipped in vinegar. Place the lid and ring on each jar and hand tighten.

4. Process in a pressure canner at 10 PSI or according to your elevation and canner type. Process quart jars for 90 minutes and pint jars for 75 minutes.

INGREDIENT TIP: *For a more traditional version of this Greek favorite, use a skillet to brown 28 skin-on chicken legs in batches in olive oil over medium-high heat. Then add 4 to 6 legs per quart jar prior to covering with the tomato pea mixture and process as instructed.*

Herbed White Beans and Chorizo Stew

This Spanish stew is the perfect blend of fresh herbs and protein, providing sustenance and dense flavor. Spanish chorizo is typically flavored with pimento, paprika, and fresh thyme and oregano. Feel free to use your favorite chorizo, bratwurst, or Italian sausage to create this hearty meal.

PREP TIME: **25 minutes** **COOK TIME:** **20 minutes**
PROCESS TIME: **90 or 75 minutes** **YIELD:** **7 quarts or 14 pints**

DIRECTIONS

1. Thoroughly rinse the dried beans in a colander, being sure to remove any rocks, debris, or disfigured beans. Place the beans in a stockpot and cover them with water. Using your hands, agitate the beans in the water to remove any dirt. Empty the beans into the colander and rinse them again. If you're using canned beans, empty them into a colander and rinse.

2. Heat the oil in a large stockpot over medium-high heat. Working in batches, add the chorizo rounds in a single layer and brown them on both sides. Add the onion and celery and cook them for about 5 minutes or until the onion is soft. Add the tomatoes, peppers, thyme, oregano, rosemary, paprika, broth, and water, and bring it to a boil. Add the cannellini beans and mix well. Reduce the heat and simmer the bean mixture for 15 minutes, stirring often. Using tongs, remove the fresh herb sprigs from the stockpot. Strip the leaves off the sprigs and place them into the stockpot, discarding the stems.

3. Using a funnel and slotted spoon, evenly distribute the meat-and-bean mixture to ¾ full in each jar. Next, ladle the stew liquid into each jar, leaving 1 inch of headspace. Remove any trapped air pockets and add additional liquid to maintain the 1-inch headspace.

4. Wipe the jar rims with a washcloth dipped in vinegar. Place the lid and ring on each jar and hand tighten.

5. Process in a pressure canner at 10 PSI or according to your elevation and canner type. Process quart jars for 90 minutes and pint jars for 75 minutes.

INGREDIENTS

2 lbs. dried cannellini beans (3 cups) or 6 (15 oz.) cans cannellini beans

3 T. olive oil

3 lbs. chorizo, cut into 1-inch rounds (6 cups)

1 Spanish onion, diced (2 cups)

4 celery ribs, diced (1 cup)

6 Roma tomatoes, diced (2 cups)

2 medium bell peppers, chopped (2 cups)

4 sprigs fresh thyme

4 sprigs fresh oregano

2 sprigs fresh rosemary

2 T. paprika

8 cups vegetable or chicken broth

4 cups water

Italian Wedding Soup

Traditional Italian wedding soup is a marriage of flavors, hence its fitting name. Filled with vegetables, flavorful broth, and delicious meatballs, this soup is truly a meal in a jar. Top with shaved Parmesan cheese and serve with a side of warm focaccia.

PREP TIME: 40 minutes **COOK TIME:** 30 minutes
PROCESS TIME: 90 or 75 minutes **YIELD:** 7 quarts or 14 pints

INGREDIENTS

Meatballs

1¼ lb. lean ground beef

1 lb. ground Italian pork sausage, sweet or spicy

2 egg yolks

½ cup grated Parmesan cheese

½ cup Italian breadcrumbs or panko

1 T. fresh parsley, finely chopped

2 tsp. fresh oregano leaves, finely chopped

4 garlic cloves, minced

½ tsp. salt (optional)

¼ tsp. black pepper

Soup Base

2 T. olive oil

1 large onion, diced (1½ cups)

6 garlic cloves, minced

3 medium carrots, diced (1½ cups)

4 celery ribs, diced (1 cup)

8 cups chicken stock

4 cups beef stock

4 cups water

10 oz. frozen spinach

DIRECTIONS

1. Preheat the oven to 450°F (232°C) and place the rack in the top third of the oven. Line a rimmed baking sheet with aluminum foil or use an oven-safe baking rack inside the baking sheet.

2. Mix the ground beef, ground pork, egg yolks, Parmesan, breadcrumbs, parsley, oregano, garlic, salt (if using), and pepper. Form the meat mixture into 1-inch balls, yielding about 80 to 90 meatballs. Line the meatballs onto the baking sheet in a single layer and place it in the oven.

3. Bake the meatballs for 8 to 10 minutes or until they are firm. Turn on the broiler and broil the meatballs for 5 minutes or until they are browned. Remove from heat and set them aside.

4. Place the oil, onion, and garlic in a large stockpot. Cook the ingredients over medium-high heat for about 5 minutes or until the onion is soft, stirring often. Add the carrots and celery and continue to cook the vegetables for an additional 5 minutes. Add the chicken stock, beef stock, water, and the frozen spinach and bring to a boil for about 10 minutes or until the spinach is fully dispersed.

5. Evenly distribute the meatballs within each jar, about 10 to 13 per quart jar and 5 to 6 per pint jar. Using a funnel, ladle soup base into each jar, leaving 1 inch of headspace.

6. Wipe the jar rims with a washcloth dipped in vinegar. Place the lid and ring on each jar and hand tighten.

7. Process in a pressure canner at 10 PSI or according to your elevation and canner type. Process quart jars for 90 minutes and pint jars for 75 minutes.

Lamb Chilindrón

Chilindrón originates from central Spain and can be made with any array of meat or poultry. Pheasant, rabbit, venison, and chicken are just a few of the variations. When substituting your favorite meat, be sure to choose an appropriate stock and wine. Using roasted red peppers is essential, whether freshly roasted, home canned, or store bought.

PREP TIME: 30 minutes   **COOK TIME: 90 minutes**
PROCESS TIME: 90 or 75 minutes   **YIELD: 7 quarts or 14 pints**

DIRECTIONS

1. Heat the oil in a large stockpot over medium-high heat. Working in batches, add the lamb to the stockpot, sprinkle with salt and pepper, and brown each side for about 2 to 3 minutes, being careful not to overcrowd the stockpot. Set the lamb aside.

2. Add the onions, pancetta, and garlic to the stockpot, scrape up the meat bits from browning, and cook the ingredients for 5 minutes. Slowly add the wine and deglaze the pot, scraping anything stuck on its base. Bring it to a rapid boil for about 30 minutes or until the wine is reduced down by half, stirring often to avoid scorching.

3. Add the beef stock, paprika, roasted bell peppers, tomatoes, parsley, rosemary, and browned lamb. Return it to a boil, then reduce the heat to low and simmer the stew for 30 minutes, stirring often.

4. Using a funnel, ladle stew into each jar, leaving 1 inch of headspace. Remove any trapped air pockets and add additional stew to maintain the 1-inch headspace.

5. Wipe the jar rims with a washcloth dipped in vinegar. Place the lid and ring on each jar and hand tighten.

6. Process in a pressure canner at 10 PSI or according to your elevation and canner type. Process quart jars for 90 minutes and pint jars for 75 minutes.

INGREDIENTS

3 T. olive oil

4 lbs. deboned lamb shoulder, cut into 2-inch pieces (12 cups)

1 tsp. salt (optional)

½ tsp. black pepper

2 sweet onions, diced (4 cups)

1 cup thick-cut pancetta or Spanish chorizo, diced

12 garlic cloves, minced

2 cups red wine

2 cups beef stock

¼ cup sweet or smoked paprika

10 red bell peppers, roasted and sliced

9 Roma tomatoes, diced (3 cups)

1 bunch fresh parsley, chopped (1 cup)

4 sprigs fresh rosemary, chopped (2 T.)

Lemon Garlic Chicken

Enjoy the flavor of lemon and garlic in this simplistic yet delicious canning recipe. Season with fresh herbs and a bit of chicken stock. This is a family favorite we enjoy any time of the year. Not a fan of rosemary? Feel free to use fresh oregano or thyme or any combination that suits your liking.

PREP TIME: 15 minutes   **COOK TIME:** None
PROCESS TIME: 90 or 75 minutes   **YIELD:** 5 quarts or 10 pints

INGREDIENTS

40 boneless, skinless 4 oz. chicken thighs, excess fat removed

2 lemons, thinly sliced and seeds removed

2 bunches of scallions, chopped

1 head garlic, peeled and minced

7 sprigs fresh rosemary, finely chopped (7 tsp.)

1 tsp. salt (optional)

1 tsp. black pepper

4 cups chicken stock

½ cup lemon juice

DIRECTIONS

1. Using your hands, mix together the chicken thighs, lemon slices, scallions, garlic, rosemary, salt, and pepper in a large bowl.

2. Raw pack the chicken into jars, placing about 8 coated thighs per quart jar or 4 coated thighs per pint, leaving a generous 1-inch headspace. Be sure to evenly distribute into each jar the lemon slices and other remnants from the bowl.

3. In a mixing bowl, whisk together the chicken stock and lemon juice. Using a funnel, ladle the stock into each jar, leaving 1 inch of headspace. Remove any trapped air pockets and add additional stock to maintain the 1-inch headspace.

4. Wipe the jar rims with a washcloth dipped in vinegar. Place the lid and ring on each jar and hand tighten.

5. Process in a pressure canner at 10 PSI or according to your elevation and canner type. Process quart jars for 90 minutes and pint jars for 75 minutes.

Tolosa Red Bean Stew

In northern Spain there's a small town south of San Sebastián called Tolosa that is known for a stew made from the red beans that grow in the region, alubias rojas Tolosarras. *Enjoy a similar version of a regional favorite using cabbage, chorizo, and sweet or smoky sausage.*

PREP TIME: 80 minutes **COOK TIME:** 45 minutes
PROCESS TIME: 90 or 75 minutes **YIELD:** 7 quarts or 14 pints

DIRECTIONS

1. Thoroughly rinse the dried beans in a colander, being sure to remove any rocks, debris, or disfigured beans. Place the beans in a stockpot and cover them with water. Bring it to a boil over high heat, and allow the beans to boil for 10 minutes. Remove from heat, cover the stockpot, and steep the beans for 1 hour.

2. Place the oil, onion, and garlic in a separate stockpot and cook them over medium-high heat for about 10 minutes or until the onion is translucent. Add the ground sausage, mix, and cook it for about 5 minutes or until it is no longer pink. Add the salt pork and chorizo and cook the ingredients for an additional 5 minutes.

3. Empty the steeped beans (or canned beans) into a colander in the sink and quickly rinse them. Add the beans, broth, water, cabbage, paprika, and oregano to the stockpot and mix well. Bring it to a boil, then reduce the heat and simmer for 15 minutes.

4. Using a funnel and slotted spoon, evenly distribute the meat and vegetables into each jar. Next, ladle the stew liquid into each jar, leaving 1 inch of headspace. Remove any trapped air pockets and add additional liquid if necessary to maintain the 1-inch headspace.

5. Wipe the jar rims with a washcloth dipped in vinegar. Place the lid and ring on each jar and hand tighten.

6. Process in a pressure canner at 10 PSI or according to your elevation and canner type. Process quart jars for 90 minutes and pint jars for 75 minutes.

INGREDIENTS

2 lbs. dried *alubias rojas Tolosarras* or dried kidney beans (4 cups), or 8 (15 oz.) cans kidney beans

3 T. olive oil

1 Spanish onion, diced (2 cups)

1 head garlic, peeled and chopped

½ lb. ground sausage, sweet or smoky

10 oz. salt pork, cut into ½-inch cubes (2 cups)

3 lbs. chorizo, cut into 1-inch rounds (6 cups)

8 cups beef broth

6 cups water

2 heads green cabbage, chopped (12 cups)

2 T. paprika

1 T. dried oregano

Moroccan Chicken with Chickpeas and Apricots

This fragrant Moroccan classic is the perfect combination of earthy and sweet. Packed with protein, it is a flavorful and filling meal in a jar. Enjoy served over a bed of couscous or alongside roasted potatoes and a side salad. It is a favorite for me and my daughter when served over brown rice.

PREP TIME: 15 minutes   **COOK TIME:** 40 minutes
PROCESS TIME: 90 or 75 minutes   **YIELD:** 5 quarts or 10 pints

INGREDIENTS

2 T. olive oil

20 boneless, skinless 4 oz. chicken thighs

1 medium red onion, diced (2 cups)

12 garlic cloves, coarsely chopped

2-inch gingerroot, peeled and grated (2 T.)

4 cups chicken broth

4 cups chickpeas, home canned or store bought, drained and rinsed

6 Roma tomatoes, diced (2 cups)

2 cups dried apricots, coarsely chopped

1 T. ground cinnamon

1 T. coriander

1 T. ground cumin

2 tsp. ground turmeric

DIRECTIONS

1. Heat the oil in a large stockpot over medium-high heat. Working in batches, add chicken to the stockpot and brown each side for about 5 minutes, being careful not to overcrowd the stockpot. Set the chicken aside.

2. Add the onion, garlic, and ginger and cook them for about 8 minutes or until the onion is soft. Add the broth, chickpeas, tomatoes, apricots, cinnamon, coriander, cumin, turmeric, and browned chicken and mix well. Cook the chickpea mixture for an additional 10 minutes.

3. Using tongs, place 4 chicken thighs in each quart jar, and 2 chicken thighs to each pint. Using a funnel, ladle the chickpea mixture into each jar, leaving 1 inch of headspace. Remove any trapped air pockets and add additional mixture to maintain the 1-inch headspace.

4. Wipe the jar rims with a washcloth dipped in vinegar. Place the lid and ring on each jar and hand tighten.

5. Process in a pressure canner at 10 PSI or according to your elevation and canner type. Process quart jars for 90 minutes and pint jars for 75 minutes.

Traditional Mediterranean Lamb Stew

Considered to be an economical dish derived from Ireland, this Mediterranean stew is anything but. Flavored and cooked to perfection, an otherwise boring lamb shoulder is transformed into a delicious meal with hints of cumin and cinnamon. The secret is using roasted tomatoes to give it a wonderful smoky flavor.

PREP TIME: 30 minutes **COOK TIME:** 45 minutes
PROCESS TIME: 90 or 75 minutes **YIELD:** 4 quarts or 8 pints

INGREDIENTS

15 Roma tomatoes (5 cups)

2 T. olive oil, divided

3 lbs. boneless lamb shoulder or stew meat (10 cups)

1 yellow onion, diced (1½ cups)

2 celery ribs, chopped (½ cup)

6 garlic cloves, minced

5 large carrots, peeled and chopped (4 cups)

4 cups beef stock

4 cups water

1 (6 oz.) can tomato paste

2 bay leaves

2 tsp. cumin

1 tsp. dried thyme

1 tsp. cinnamon (optional)

1 tsp. salt (optional)

½ tsp. black pepper

DIRECTIONS

1. Wash and core your tomatoes. Using a paring knife, place two lengthwise slits into the skin of each tomato and line them onto a deep-walled cookie sheet. Drizzle 1 tablespoon of olive oil over the top of the tomatoes and place the sheet on your top rack in the oven. Broil for 10 minutes or until you start to see the tomatoes start to blacken. Shut off the broiler and keep the tomatoes in the oven.

2. Heat the remaining oil in a large stockpot over medium-high heat. Working in batches, add the lamb to the stockpot and brown each side for about 2 to 3 minutes, being careful not to overcrowd the stockpot. Set the lamb aside.

3. Add a splash of beef stock into the pot and deglaze the pan, scraping all the meat bits from the bottom of the pot. Add the onion, celery, and garlic. Mix well and cook the ingredients for about 8 minutes or until the onion is translucent.

4. Remove the tomatoes from the oven. Gently remove excess char from the tomatoes and discard the char. Add the tomatoes to the stockpot and mix well. Bring the tomato mixture to a boil, crushing the tomatoes periodically.

> **After you process your jars, don't forget to store them with the rings removed.**

5. Add the carrots, browned meat, beef stock, water, tomato paste, bay leaves, cumin, thyme, cinnamon (if using), salt (if using), and black pepper to the pot and return it to a boil. Reduce the heat and simmer the stew for 15 minutes, stirring often to blend and avoid scorching. Remove and discard the bay leaves.

6. Using a funnel and slotted spoon, evenly distribute the meat and vegetables into each jar. Next, ladle the stew liquid into each jar, leaving 1 inch of headspace. Remove any trapped air pockets and add additional liquid if necessary to maintain the 1-inch headspace.

7. Wipe the jar rims with a washcloth dipped in vinegar. Place the lid and ring on each jar and hand tighten.

8. Process in a pressure canner at 10 PSI or according to your elevation and canner type. Process quart jars for 90 minutes and pint jars for 75 minutes.

INGREDIENT TIP: *If you would like to enhance the flavor of the stew, add 1 cup of red wine. To do so, reduce the water to 3 cups and add the wine to the pot with the stock and water in step 5 of the instructions.*

Zuppa Toscana

This very popular soup is a traditional Italian soup often consumed in the colder winter months. It boasts a high nutritional value and is hearty in nature. Authentically made with cream and Parmesan cheese, we will create and preserve the soup with all its goodness and leave the addition of cream and cheese for when you're ready to pop open a jar lid to heat and serve. Instructions to do so are in the recipe tip.

PREP TIME: 30 minutes   COOK TIME: 40 minutes
PROCESS TIME: 75 or 60 minutes   YIELD: 7 quarts or 14 pints

INGREDIENTS

1 lb. bacon, cut into 1-inch pieces

3 T. olive oil

2 sweet onions, diced (4 cups)

1 head garlic, peeled and minced

3 lbs. Italian ground sausage

12 cups chicken stock

6 cups water

12 medium potatoes, peeled and cut into ½-inch cubes (12 cups)

2 lbs. kale, destemmed and chopped (12 cups)

½ T. red pepper flakes

1 tsp. black pepper

DIRECTIONS

1. Place the bacon in a skillet and cook it for about 8 to 10 minutes or until the bacon is crisp but not burnt. Set the bacon aside to cool, then use your fingers to break it into crumbles.

2. Place the oil, onion, and garlic in a large stockpot and heat them over medium-high heat for 10 minutes or until the onion is translucent. Add the sausage and cook it for 15 minutes or until it is fully cooked.

3. Add the bacon crumbles, stock, water, potatoes, kale, red pepper flakes, and pepper to the stockpot and mix well. Bring it to a boil, then reduce the heat and simmer the soup, for 5 minutes.

4. Using a funnel and slotted spoon, evenly distribute the meat and vegetables into each jar. Next, ladle the soup broth into each jar, leaving 1 inch of headspace. Remove any trapped air pockets and add additional broth if necessary to maintain the 1-inch headspace.

5. Wipe the jar rims with a washcloth dipped in vinegar. Place the lid and ring on each jar and hand tighten.

6. Process in a pressure canner at 10 PSI or according to your elevation and canner type. Process quart jars for 75 minutes and pint jars for 60 minutes.

RECIPE TIP: *When ready to heat and serve, bring soup to a boil and slowly add 1 cup of half-and-half or heavy whipping cream to each quart (or ½ cup to each pint) and heat through. Serve hot and top with a generous helping of shredded Parmesan cheese.*

Asian Cuisine

Welcome to the wonderful world of Asian cuisine! From the fragrant curries of India to the bold and spicy dishes of Southeast Asia, Asian cuisine is a treasure trove of exotic flavors, aromas, and textures that have captivated food lovers around the globe for centuries.

At the heart of Asian cuisine is a rich and diverse culinary tradition that has been shaped by centuries of history, cultural exchange, and innovation. Whether you're a fan of bulgogi, curried dishes, or popular Thai cuisine, you'll find that each region of Asia has its own unique culinary style and flavor profile that is sure to delight your senses.

The history of Asian cuisine dates back thousands of years, with each country and region having its unique culinary traditions and flavors. Chinese cuisine is one of the oldest and most diverse, with a rich history that includes the use of ingredients such as rice, soy sauce, and tofu. Japanese cuisine is also steeped in tradition and is known for its emphasis on fresh, seasonal ingredients and delicate flavors. Indian cuisine is known for its vibrant spices and herbs as well as both vegetarian and non-vegetarian dishes.

Asian cuisine has also gained popularity in recent years due to the increased availability of international ingredients and a growing interest in cultural exchange and exploration through food. As a result, Asian cuisine has become an important part of many people's diets and a beloved cuisine around the world.

In this chapter, we'll explore fun ingredients, techniques, and cultural influences that have shaped this rich and vibrant cuisine. We'll introduce you to some of the most iconic dishes from various regions of Asia, including China, Japan, Thailand, India, and Vietnam.

Chinese Daikon Radish Dinner

Daikon, or white radish, is a common element in Asian cuisine. A white, crunchy root vegetable with a sweet and peppery flavor, it provides texture and flavor to any dish or salad. Enjoy this amazing meal with chicken, turkey, beef, or pork. It stands alone or may be served alongside steamed rice.

PREP TIME: 15 minutes   COOK TIME: 25 minutes
PROCESS TIME: 90 or 75 minutes   YIELD: 4 quarts or 8 pints

DIRECTIONS

1. Place the oil, green onions, and ginger in a large stockpot and cook them over medium-high heat for 5 minutes, stirring often. Add the ground meat and cook it for about 15 minutes or until the meat is cooked through. Add the hoisin paste, radishes, stock, five-spice, and sugar. Mix well and bring it to a boil, then reduce the heat and simmer the mixture for 5 minutes.

2. Using a funnel, ladle the mixture into each jar, leaving a 1-inch headspace. Remove any trapped air pockets and add additional mixture as necessary to maintain the 1-inch headspace. Be sure to add additional stock to cover the mixture and maintain the headspace.

3. Wipe the jar rims with a washcloth dipped in vinegar. Place the lid and ring on each jar and hand tighten.

4. Process in a pressure canner at 10 PSI or according to your elevation and canner type. Process quart jars for 90 minutes and pint jars for 75 minutes.

INGREDIENT TIP: *If you do not have access to hoisin paste, feel free to substitute with 3 tablespoons of soy sauce and 3 tablespoons of dry white wine.*

INGREDIENTS

2 T. vegetable oil

2 bunches green onions, diced

2-inch gingerroot, peeled and minced (2 T.)

3 lbs. ground meat (chicken, turkey, beef, or pork)

3 T. hoisin paste

6 lbs. daikon radish, peeled and chopped in 1-inch pieces (10 cups)

8 cups stock (beef, chicken or vegetable)

1 T. Chinese five-spice

1 T. granulated sugar

Curried Salmon

Creating this creamy and flavorful recipe gives you the ability to have a ready-made meal in minutes. Canned coconut milk provides this Thai dish with its creamy texture while the red curry paste and ginger boost its delicious flavor. Heat a jarful in a saucepan and serve over rice or over ramen noodles.

PREP TIME: 15 minutes   **COOK TIME:** 10 minutes
PROCESS TIME: 160 or 110 minutes   **YIELD:** 6 quarts, or 12 pints, or 24 half pints

INGREDIENTS

12 lbs. salmon filet

3 medium red bell peppers, cored and diced

1 sweet onion, sliced (2 cups)

1 T. vegetable oil

3-inch gingerroot, peeled and minced (3 T.)

4 T. red curry paste

3 (13.5 oz.) cans unsweetened coconut milk

3 T. soy sauce

2 T. dark brown sugar (optional)

DIRECTIONS

1. Cut the salmon filet to the size jar you are using, leaving a generous 1-inch headspace. Raw pack the filets, red bell pepper, and onion, maintaining the generous 1-inch headspace.

2. Place the oil and ginger in a deep skillet and sauté over medium-high heat for 1 minute, stirring often. Add the curry paste, coconut milk, soy sauce, and sugar (if using). Stirring constantly, heat the sauce for about 8 to 10 minutes or until the thick coconut milk begins to thin out and the ingredients are well blended.

3. Using a funnel, slowly ladle the hot sauce into each jar, leaving 1 inch of headspace. Remove any air pockets and add additional sauce as necessary to maintain the 1-inch headspace.

4. Wipe the jar rims with a washcloth dipped in vinegar. Place the lid and ring on each jar and hand tighten.

5. Process in a pressure canner at 10 PSI or according to your elevation and canner type. Process quart jars for 160 minutes and pint and half-pint jars for 110 minutes.

INGREDIENT TIP: *Approximately 1 pound of salmon will fit one pint jar depending on its thickness and how it is cut. Feel free to scale this recipe up to accommodate the number of jars you'd like to yield based on the amount of salmon you have to preserve.*

Korean Bulgogi

This version of Korean bulgogi is an absolute delight, and having jars of its yummy goodness sitting in your pantry will make meal prep a cinch! Ground beef simmered in a delicious sauce made from ginger, red pepper flakes, and a bit of sesame oil will brighten up an otherwise dull day. Serve with rice and top with sliced green onions or use in your favorite Asian dish.

PREP TIME: 10 minutes   COOK TIME: 35 minutes
PROCESS TIME: 90 or 75 minutes   YIELD: 5 quarts or 10 pints

DIRECTIONS

1. Place the ground beef in a stockpot and cook it over medium-high heat for about 20 minutes or until browned. Drain the grease in a colander and return the cooked beef to stockpot.

2. Add the brown sugar, soy sauce, garlic, sesame oil, ginger, red pepper flakes, and sesame seeds. Mix well and cook the mixture for an additional 15 minutes.

3. Using a funnel, ladle the bulgogi into jars and pack down using your headspace-measuring tool, leaving 1 inch of headspace.

4. Wipe the jar rims with a washcloth dipped in vinegar. Place the lid and ring on each jar and hand tighten.

5. Process in a pressure canner at 10 PSI or according to your elevation and canner type. Process quart jars for 90 minutes and pint jars for 75 minutes.

RECIPE TIP: *Upon cooling, the naturally remaining fat will solidify in the jar, often near the top. This is completely normal and may remain or be removed when popping a jar lid to heat and eat the meal.*

INGREDIENTS

12 lbs. ground beef

1 cup packed brown sugar

1 cup soy sauce

2 heads garlic, minced (½ cup)

4 T. sesame oil

3-inch gingerroot, peeled and minced (3 T.)

1 to 2 T. red pepper flakes

1 T. sesame seeds

Caramel Chicken or Shrimp

This Vietnamese-inspired dish is a combination of spicy, sweet, and salty and it boasts a gorgeous caramel color, hence its name. This recipe can be made with either bone-in or boneless thighs, and you may leave some of the skin on the thigh if you prefer. Heat a jarful in a skillet and serve this delicious meal over a bed of Jasmine rice with a side of steamed broccoli.

PREP TIME: 10 minutes **COOK TIME:** 30 minutes
PROCESS TIME: 90 or 75 minutes **YIELD:** 5 quarts or 10 pints

INGREDIENTS

3 T. vegetable oil, divided

35 to 40 boneless, skinless 4 oz. chicken thighs or 5 lbs. medium shrimp

3 jalapeños, cored and sliced into thin rounds

12 garlic cloves, minced

1 cup honey

1 cup water

¾ cup soy sauce, or fish sauce

½ cup rice vinegar

½ cup oyster sauce

DIRECTIONS

1. Heat 1 tablespoon of the oil in a skillet over medium-high heat. Working in batches, add the chicken to the skillet and brown each side for about 8 minutes or until both sides are golden brown and slightly crispy, being careful not to overcrowd the stockpot. Remove from heat.

2. Using tongs, tightly pack the thighs into each jar—about 7 or 8 thighs per quart jar and 3 to 4 per pint jar, depending on their size—leaving a generous 1 inch of headspace. Evenly distribute the jalapeños and garlic among the jars.

3. In a bowl, whisk together the honey, water, soy sauce, vinegar, and oyster sauce. Using a funnel, ladle the sauce into each jar, leaving 1 inch of headspace. Remove any trapped air pockets and add additional sauce if necessary to maintain the 1-inch headspace.

4. Wipe the jar rims with a washcloth dipped in vinegar. Place the lid and ring on each jar and hand tighten.

5. Process in a pressure canner at 10 PSI or according to your elevation and canner type. If using bone-in chicken thighs, process quart jars for 75 minutes and pint jars for 65 minutes. If using boneless chicken thighs, process quart jars for 90 minutes and pint jars for 75 minutes. If using shrimp, process quart jars for 55 minutes and pint jars for 45 minutes.

INGREDIENT TIP: *If you'd prefer to make this recipe using raw, peeled, and deveined shrimp, simply pack the cleaned shrimp into each jar, leaving 1 inch of headspace. Cover the shrimp with the caramel sauce, maintaining the 1-inch headspace.*

Kung Pao Chicken

Kung pao chicken is believed to be named after Ding Baozhen (1820 to 1886), the Qing dynasty official and governor of Sichuan Province. This Sichuanese staple was brought over to America, making it a well-known favorite at Chinese restaurants. Sticking with its westernized flavor, enjoy this deliciously beautiful version on your pantry shelf year after year.

PREP TIME: 20 minutes **COOK TIME:** 21 minutes
PROCESS TIME: 90 or 75 minutes **YIELD:** 5 quarts or 10 pints

DIRECTIONS

1. Place the soy sauce, vinegar, oil, and ginger in a bowl and whisk them together. Add the chicken pieces to the bowl and mix to coat the chicken. Cover the bowl and let the chicken marinate at room temperature for 30 minutes or, for the best results, marinate it in the refrigerator for 2 hours.

2. Place the chicken and marinade into a stockpot. Cook the chicken on medium-high heat for 3 minutes on each side. Add the peppers, onion, celery, and cashews, and heat it for about 5 minutes or until heated all the way through, stirring to coat the ingredients in the marinade.

3. In a bowl, whisk together the water, hoisin sauce, and sugar, then add the mixture to the stockpot. Mix well and bring it to a boil. Reduce the heat and simmer the mixture for 10 minutes, then remove from heat.

4. Using a funnel and slotted spoon, evenly distribute the chicken and vegetables into each jar, filling to roughly ¾ full. Next, ladle the sauce into each jar, leaving a generous 1 inch of headspace. Remove any trapped air pockets and add additional sauce to maintain the generous 1-inch headspace.

5. Wipe the jar rims with a washcloth dipped in vinegar. Place the lid and ring on each jar and hand tighten.

6. Process in a pressure canner at 10 PSI or according to your elevation and canner type. Process quart jars for 90 minutes and pint jars for 75 minutes.

INGREDIENTS

¼ cup soy sauce

¼ cup rice wine vinegar

¼ cup sesame oil

2-inch gingerroot, peeled and minced (2 T.)

5 lbs. boneless, skinless chicken breasts, cut into 2-inch pieces (15 cups)

6 red bell peppers, cored and chopped (7 cups)

1 sweet onion, chopped (2 cups)

4 celery ribs, chopped (1 cup)

1 cup roasted unsalted cashews or peanuts

4 cups water

4 T. hoisin sauce

¼ cup sugar

Lemongrass Chicken Soup

Lemongrass is a key ingredient in Southeast Asian dishes, specifically Thai and Vietnamese cuisines. Known for its citrusy flavor and lemony aroma, use the bottom third of its woody stem when cooking and canning. Feel free to substitute lemongrass paste if you do not have access to fresh lemongrass stalks.

PREP TIME: 20 minutes   **COOK TIME:** 30 minutes
PROCESS TIME: 90 or 75 minutes   **YIELD:** 5 quarts or 10 pints

INGREDIENTS

3 T. vegetable oil

6 boneless, skinless 4 oz. chicken thighs (2 cups)

4 boneless, skinless 8 oz. chicken breasts (5 cups)

1 cup finely chopped shallots

2-inch gingerroot, peeled and minced (2 T.)

6 garlic cloves, minced

8 stalks lemongrass, chopped

12 cups chicken broth

¼ cup fish sauce

½ head cabbage, shredded (3 cups)

4 carrots, chopped (2 cups)

8 oz. button mushrooms, rough chopped (optional)

3 tsp. red chili paste (optional)

DIRECTIONS

1. Heat the oil in a large stockpot over medium-high heat. Working in batches, add the chicken to the stockpot and cook each side for about 5 minutes, being careful not to overcrowd the stockpot. Set the chicken aside to cool. Add the shallots, ginger, garlic, and lemongrass to the stockpot, mixing and scraping up all the bits from cooking the chicken. Cook the mixture for 5 minutes or until the shallots have softened.

2. Slowly add the chicken broth and deglaze the pot. When the chicken has cooled, cut it into 1-inch pieces and return it to the stockpot. Add the fish sauce, cabbage, carrots, mushrooms, and chili paste. Mix well and bring it to a boil, then reduce the heat to simmer. Simmer the soup for 15 minutes, then remove from heat.

3. Using a funnel, ladle the soup into each jar, leaving 1 inch of headspace.

4. Wipe the jar rims with a washcloth dipped in vinegar. Place the lid and ring on each jar and hand tighten.

5. Process in a pressure canner at 10 PSI or according to your elevation and canner type. Process quart jars for 90 minutes and pint jars for 75 minutes.

Mango Beef with Thai Curry

Known in Thai as gaeng garee *or* kaeng kari, *yellow curry is one of the most well-known curries in Thai cuisine. Earthy spice with a touch of sweet is the best way to describe this delicious dish. Serve it hot in a bowl of rice topped with chopped green onions and a lime wedge.*

PREP TIME: 30 minutes   **COOK TIME:** 50 minutes
PROCESS TIME: 90 or 75 minutes   **YIELD:** 7 quarts or 14 pints

INGREDIENTS

- 4 lbs. beef chuck top blade or chuck roast, cut crosswise into ¼-inch thick slices
- 12 cups water
- 2 (13.5 oz.) cans unsweetened coconut milk
- 6 to 8 T. yellow Thai curry paste
- 3 T. tamarind paste
- 2-inch gingerroot, peeled and finely chopped (2 T.)
- 3 cups diced mango, fresh or frozen
- 3 red bell peppers, cored and sliced (3 cups)
- 1 red onion, sliced (2½ cups)
- 4 carrots, peeled and chopped (2 cups)

DIRECTIONS

1. Place the beef and water in a large stockpot and bring it to a boil over medium-high heat. Reduce the heat to a rapid simmer for 20 minutes or until the beef is fork tender. Skim off and discard any foam. Add the coconut milk, curry paste, tamarind paste, and ginger and mix well. Return the mixture to a rapid simmer for an additional 20 minutes, stirring often.

2. Add the remaining ingredients, mix well, and simmer for an additional 10 minutes.

3. Using a funnel and slotted spoon, evenly distribute the meat and vegetables into each jar, leaving a generous 1¼-inch headspace. Next, ladle curry sauce into each jar, leaving 1 inch of headspace. Remove any trapped air pockets and add additional sauce if necessary to maintain the 1-inch headspace.

4. Wipe the jar rims with a washcloth dipped in vinegar. Place the lid and ring on each jar and hand tighten.

5. Process in a pressure canner at 10 PSI or according to your elevation and canner type. Process quart jars for 90 minutes and pint jars for 75 minutes.

RECIPE TIP: *If you prefer to add a bit of heat to your recipe, feel free to add 3 to 5 tablespoons of red curry paste, or according to your heat tolerance.*

Oxtail Soup

With versions spanning many cultures, this Chinese staple is as hearty as it is delicious. Made from beef tails, its nutrient-rich broth is high in protein, collagen, calcium, and iron. Enjoy a hot bowl atop rice noodles and topped with chopped cilantro.

PREP TIME: 10 minutes   COOK TIME: 60 minutes
PROCESS TIME: 90 or 75 minutes   YIELD: 5 quarts or 10 pints

DIRECTIONS

1. Preheat the oven to 425°F (218°C).

2. Line a cookie sheet with the oxtails. Using a silicone spatula, spread tomato paste onto each oxtail. Place the cookie sheet on the middle rack and roast the oxtails for 30 minutes. Remove from oven and set them aside.

3. Place the oil and onion in a large stockpot and cook the onions over medium-high heat for about 10 minutes or until they are translucent. Add the water, broth, soy sauce, radishes, garlic, and oxtails and bring it to a boil, mixing often. Reduce the heat and simmer the soup for 20 minutes, stirring often.

4. Using a funnel and slotted spoon, evenly distribute the oxtails and radishes in each jar. Next, ladle the soup into each jar, leaving 1 inch of headspace.

5. Wipe the jar rims with a washcloth dipped in vinegar. Place the lid and ring on each jar and hand tighten.

6. Process in a pressure canner at 10 PSI or according to your elevation and canner type. Process quart jars for 90 minutes and pint jars for 75 minutes.

INGREDIENTS

6 lbs. oxtails, cut at the joint to 1½-inch thick rounds

1 (6 oz.) can tomato paste

2 T. vegetable oil

2 yellow onions, sliced (1½ cups)

10 cups water

4 cups beef broth

¼ cup soy sauce (optional)

3 lbs. Daikon radish or turnips, chopped into 1-inch pieces (5 cups)

6 garlic cloves, smashed

Chana Masala

This popular North Indian dish originating in the Punjab region is made with chickpeas, tomatoes, and an array of spices that tantalize your tastebuds. Canners may create an extremely spicy or mild version based on your personal liking. Enjoy this protein-packed recipe sprinkled with a bit of chopped cilantro and a lemon wedge.

PREP TIME: 85 minutes   **COOK TIME:** 25 minutes
PROCESS TIME: 90 or 75 minutes   **YIELD:** 5 quarts or 10 pints

INGREDIENTS

6 cups dried chickpeas

15 Roma tomatoes, diced (5 cups)

4 cups water

2 sweet onions, diced (4 cups)

2-inch gingerroot, peeled and minced (2 T.)

1 to 3 T. Kashmiri red chili powder (adjust to taste)

1 T. garam masala

2 tsp. salt

2 tsp. ground cinnamon

1 tsp. turmeric

1 tsp. dried mango powder (optional)

DIRECTIONS

1. Thoroughly rinse the dried chickpeas in a colander, being sure to remove any rocks, debris, or disfigured beans. Place the chickpeas in a stockpot and cover them with water. Bring it to a boil over high heat, and allow the beans to boil for 10 minutes. Remove from heat, cover the stockpot, and steep the beans for 1 hour.

2. In a separate stockpot, add the tomatoes, water, onions, ginger, chili powder, garam masala, salt, cinnamon, turmeric, and mango powder (if using). Mix well and bring it to a boil over medium-high heat. Reduce the heat to medium and continue a rapid simmer for 15 minutes, stirring often to avoid scorching the sauce.

3. Empty the steeped chickpeas into a colander in the sink and quickly rinse them. Shake off any excess water, then add the chickpeas to the stockpot containing the tomato mixture. Return it to a rapid simmer for 10 minutes, stirring often.

4. Using a funnel, ladle the masala into each jar, leaving 1 inch of headspace. Remove any trapped air pockets and add additional sauce if necessary to maintain the 1-inch headspace.

5. Wipe the jar rims with a washcloth dipped in vinegar. Place the lid and ring on each jar and hand tighten.

6. Process in a pressure canner at 10 PSI or according to your elevation and canner type. Process quart jars for 90 minutes and pint jars for 75 minutes.

Pork and Bok Choy Soup

This authentically seasoned soup can be enjoyed in many ways. One way is to add cooked udon noodles. Some will hard-boil an egg, cut it in half, and add it to the soup upon serving. Others will add 2 ounces of kimchi upon serving to give the soup some added spice. No matter how you serve it, this meal is an amazing asset to have in your pantry.

PREP TIME: **15 minutes**   **COOK TIME:** **15 minutes**
PROCESS TIME: **90 or 75 minutes**   **YIELD:** **5 quarts or 10 pints**

DIRECTIONS

1. Place the stock, water, pork, bok choy, soy sauce, aji mirin, garlic, ginger, and sriracha in a large stockpot and mix well. Bring it to a boil over medium-high heat, then reduce the heat and simmer the soup for 5 minutes.

2. Using tongs, evenly distribute the pork slices among the jars. Next, using a funnel, ladle the soup into each jar, leaving 1 inch of headspace.

3. Wipe the jar rims with a washcloth dipped in vinegar. Place the lid and ring on each jar and hand tighten.

4. Process in a pressure canner at 10 PSI or according to your elevation and canner type. Process quart jars for 90 minutes and pint jars for 75 minutes.

INGREDIENTS

9 cups chicken stock

9 cups water

3 lbs. pork tenderloin, cut into slices ¼ inch thick

3 bok choy, coarsely chopped (15 cups)

½ cup soy sauce

½ cup aji mirin (optional)

12 garlic cloves, minced (2 T.)

3-inch gingerroot, peeled and minced (3 T.)

2 tsp. sriracha sauce

Sukiyaki

Made with fatty beef, leafy vegetables, tofu, and mushrooms, this authentically flavored meal is a must-have for every canner who enjoys Japanese cuisine. When ready to heat and eat, create a hearty dish by adding steamed rice, enoki mushrooms, egg yolks, and mung bean noodles.

PREP TIME: 30 minutes   **COOK TIME: 20 minutes**
PROCESS TIME: 90 or 75 minutes   **YIELD: 6 quarts or 12 pints**

DIRECTIONS

1. Heat the oil in a stockpot over high heat. Working in batches, add the beef to the stockpot and sear each side for about 5 seconds. Set the beef aside. Add 1 cup of the seared beef to each quart jar and ½ cup to each pint. Next, add ½ cup tofu to each quart jar and ¼ cup to each pint jar.

2. Add the green onions to the stockpot and cook them for 2 minutes, adding ½ cup of beef stock to deglaze the pan. Add the remaining stock and the bok choy, cabbage, and mushrooms to the stockpot and bring it to a boil. Allow the stock to boil for 5 minutes or until the leafy greens begin to wilt. Using a funnel and slotted spoon, evenly distribute the greens and mushrooms among the jars.

3. Add the mirin, soy sauce, sake, and brown sugar to the stockpot and return to a boil, stirring often to dissolve the sugar. Ladle stock into each jar, leaving 1 inch of headspace. Remove trapped air pockets and add additional stock if necessary to maintain the 1-inch headspace.

4. Wipe the jar rims with a washcloth dipped in vinegar. Place the lid and ring on each jar and hand tighten.

5. Process in a pressure canner at 10 PSI or according to your elevation and canner type. Process quart jars for 90 minutes and pint jars for 75 minutes.

INGREDIENTS

3 T. vegetable oil

3 lbs. chuck roast, cut thin against the grain

1 (16 oz.) block firm tofu, cut into 1-inch cubes (3 cups)

1 bunch green onions, diced (1 cup)

8 cups beef stock, divided

2 bok choy, coarsely chopped (10 cups)

1 napa cabbage, chopped (8 cups)

20 shitake mushrooms, sliced (6 cups)

1 cup mirin

1 cup soy sauce

½ cup sake

4 T. brown sugar

Punjabi Dal Makhani

Kashmiri red chili powder gives this dish its exceptional red color and a bountiful flavor with a mild spice. This popular Indian dish is perfect for those who don't eat meat yet wish to have protein in their diet. Heat it in a saucepan and add additional water to gain the consistency you wish to achieve. Feel free to add an ounce or two of coconut cream to make the dal creamier. Be sure to make buttery brown rice to mix into the dal before serving.

PREP TIME: **10 minutes**   **COOK TIME:** **30 minutes**
PROCESS TIME: **90 or 75 minutes**   **YIELD:** **5 quarts or 10 pints**

INGREDIENTS

3 T. vegetable oil

1 large yellow onion, diced (2 cups)

3-inch gingerroot, peeled and minced (3 T.)

6 garlic cloves, minced (1 T.)

15 cups water

12 Roma tomatoes, diced (4 cups)

2 T. Kashmiri red chili powder

1 T. ground coriander

1 T. ground cumin

2 tsp. garam masala

2 tsp. salt (optional)

4 cups dried brown, green, or black lentils

1 cup dried kidney beans, cleaned and rinsed

DIRECTIONS

1. Place the oil, onion, ginger, and garlic in a large stockpot and cook over medium-high heat for 10 minutes. Add the water, tomatoes, chili powder, coriander, cumin, garam masala, and salt (if using). Mix well and bring it to a boil. Reduce the heat and simmer the soup for 15 minutes. Add the lentils and kidney beans, mix well, and simmer the lentil mixture for an additional 5 minutes.

2. Using a funnel, slotted spoon, and ruler, fill each quart jar with 4 inches of the lentil mixture and each pint jar with 2 inches of lentil mixture. To measure, place the start of the ruler onto the table next to the jar and fill to the required inch mark.

3. After the solids are dispersed among the jars, ladle the hot soup broth over the solids, leaving 1 inch of headspace. Remove any trapped air pockets and add additional broth if necessary to maintain the 1-inch headspace.

4. Wipe the jar rims with a washcloth dipped in vinegar. Place the lid and ring on each jar and hand tighten.

5. Process in a pressure canner at 10 PSI or according to your elevation and canner type. Process quart jars for 90 minutes and pint jars for 75 minutes.

Szechuan Chicken

This popular Chinese dish contains plenty of spice and colorful vegetables, giving it gorgeous color and amazing flavor. While it is often served as a stir fry, this home-canned version is an amazing rendition of the popular meal. Created with authentic Sichuan peppercorns and cashew nuts, simply thicken the dish upon heating it to serve a delicious Chinese meal in minutes.

PREP TIME: 25 minutes **COOK TIME: 20 minutes**
PROCESS TIME: 90 or 75 minutes **YIELD: 5 quarts or 10 pints**

DIRECTIONS

1. Heat 1 tablespoon of the oil in a stockpot over medium-high heat. Working in batches, add the chicken to the stockpot and lightly brown one side for about 3 minutes, being careful not to overcrowd the stockpot. Remove from heat.

2. In the same stockpot, add the remaining oil, garlic, and ginger and cook them for 3 minutes. Return the browned chicken to the stockpot and toss with the garlic and ginger. Add the green and red bell peppers, carrots, celery, onion, cashews, chilies, and peppercorns to the stockpot and mix well. Remove from heat.

3. Using a funnel, ladle mixture into each jar, leaving 1 inch of headspace. Be sure to press the mixture down inside each jar to adequately maximize the jar space. In a bowl, whisk together the honey, chicken stock, soy sauce, hoisin sauce, sesame oil, and ClearJel.

4. Ladle the sauce into each jar, leaving 1 inch of headspace. Remove any trapped air pockets and add additional sauce if necessary to maintain the 1-inch headspace.

5. Wipe the jar rims with a washcloth dipped in vinegar. Place the lid and ring on each jar and hand tighten.

6. Process in a pressure canner at 10 PSI or according to your elevation and canner type. Process quart jars for 90 minutes and pint jars for 75 minutes.

INGREDIENTS

3 T. vegetable oil, divided

2½ lbs. boneless, skinless chicken breasts, cut into 1-inch cubes (5 cups)

2½ lbs. boneless, skinless chicken thighs, cut into 1-inch cubes (5 cups)

1 head garlic, peeled and minced (¼ cup)

3-inch gingerroot, peeled and minced (3 T.)

3 medium green bell peppers, chopped (3 cups)

3 medium red bell peppers, chopped (3 cups)

4 carrots, peeled and chopped diagonally (2 cups)

4 celery ribs, chopped diagonally (1½ cups)

1 large yellow onion, chopped (1½ cups)

1 cup whole cashew nuts

60 to 75 small dried red chilies

3 to 4 T. Sichuan peppercorns

1 cup honey

1 cup chicken stock

1 cup soy sauce

½ cup hoisin sauce

¼ cup sesame oil

3 T. ClearJel

Vietnamese Chicken Curry

Also called cà ri gà, this flavorful curry meal in a jar is simple and fill-ing comfort food. Made with chicken, potatoes, carrots, and a coconut curry broth, it will soon become your go-to jar. Enjoy it warmed up and served with rice noodles.

PREP TIME: 25 minutes   COOK TIME: 25 minutes
PROCESS TIME: 90 or 75 minutes   YIELD: 5 quarts or 10 pints

DIRECTIONS

1. Heat 1 tablespoon of the oil in a stockpot over medium-high heat. Working in batches, add the chicken to the stockpot and cook each side for about 8 minutes or until both sides are golden brown and slightly crispy, being careful not to overcrowd the stockpot. Remove from heat. Using tongs, tightly pack the browned chicken into each jar, about 3 or 4 thighs per quart jar and 1 to 2 per pint jar, depending on their size.

2. In the same stockpot, add any remaining oil, onion, and garlic and cook them over medium-high heat, scraping the bits off the bottom of the stockpot. Slowly add one cup of broth to the stockpot and deglaze the pan. Stir in the remaining broth and the potatoes, carrots, celery, coconut milk, curry powder, fish sauce, lemongrass, and sugar. Bring it to a boil, stirring often, and allow the broth to boil for 5 minutes.

3. Using a funnel and slotted spoon, evenly distribute the vegetables into each jar, leaving 1 inch of headspace. Next, ladle the broth over the top of the meat and vegetables, leaving 1 inch of headspace. Remove any trapped air pockets and add additional broth if necessary to main-tain the 1-inch headspace.

4. Wipe the jar rims with a washcloth dipped in vinegar. Place the lid and ring on each jar and hand tighten.

5. Process in a pressure canner at 10 PSI or according to your elevation and canner type. Process quart jars for 90 minutes and pint jars for 75 minutes.

INGREDIENT TIP: *During storage, the coconut milk may solidify and separate, which is totally normal given its naturally high oil con-tent. It will return to its creamy texture upon reheating.*

INGREDIENTS

4 T. vegetable oil, divided

17 to 20 boneless 4 oz. chicken thighs

1 medium red onion, diced (2 cups)

1 head garlic, minced (¼ cup)

12 cups chicken broth, divided

4 lbs. russet potatoes, peeled and chopped (8 cups)

6 carrots, peeled and chopped (3 cups)

4 celery ribs, diced (1 cup)

1 (13.5 oz.) can unsweetened coconut milk

¼ cup yellow curry powder

3 T. fish sauce

3 T. lemongrass paste

2 T. brown sugar

Thai Chicken Larb Gai

A popular dish in Laos and Isan, Thailand, this dish is an easy meal packed with flavor and loaded with protein. Simply heat a jar and eat it with a side of rice or use it to fill fresh lettuce wraps for a bit of crunch. Top with cilantro and a lime wedge before serving. If you need a quick 1-cup serving lunch, preserve this recipe in half pints and take it on the go.

PREP TIME: 10 minutes COOK TIME: 25 minutes
PROCESS TIME: 90 or 75 minutes
YIELD: 7 quarts, or 14 pints, or 28 half pints

INGREDIENTS

9 lbs. ground chicken (27 cups)

1 medium red onion, diced (2 cups)

2 red Thai chilies, seeded and finely chopped

6 garlic cloves, minced (1 T.)

¼ cup fresh mint leaves, finely chopped

½ cup fresh cilantro leaves, finely chopped

¼ cup lime juice

½ cup fish sauce

3 T. lemongrass paste

1 T. brown sugar

1 T. Sriracha chili sauce

DIRECTIONS

1. Place the chicken, onion, chilies, and garlic in a large stockpot and cook over medium-high heat for 15 minutes or until the chicken is cooked through, mixing often. Add the mint, cilantro, lime juice, fish sauce, lemongrass, sugar, and sriracha, mix well, and cook for an additional 10 minutes.

2. Using a funnel, fill each jar with the chicken mixture, leaving a 1-inch headspace, packing down as you fill.

3. Wipe the jar rims with a washcloth dipped in vinegar. Place the lid and ring on each jar and hand tighten.

4. Process in a pressure canner at 10 PSI or according to your elevation and canner type. Process quart jars for 90 minutes and pint and half-pint jars for 75 minutes.

INGREDIENT TIP: *Feel free to substitute ground pork or ground turkey for the chicken. Also, feel free to add additional Thai chilies if you prefer more heat.*

Canning Shrimp

Shrimp and other crustaceans are healthy proteins that are easy to preserve in jars. Oftentimes home canners will preserve shrimp on their own to later use with other recipes. Such as lemon garlic butter shrimp, shrimp linguine on the stovetop, or to create your favorite stir-fry.

PREP TIME: 25 minutes   **COOK TIME:** 25 minutes
PROCESS TIME: 90 or 75 minutes   **YIELD:** 5 quarts or 10 pints

DIRECTIONS

1. Remove heads from shrimp as soon as they are caught. Chill on ice until you are ready to pressure can. If you are using frozen raw shrimp, be sure to thaw them completely in the refrigerator before canning. Whether fresh or thawed, place the shrimp in a colander, rinse, and drain.

2. Place 1 gallon of water, the vinegar, and ½ cup of the salt in a large stockpot and bring to a boil over high heat, stirring to dissolve the salt. Add the beheaded shrimp, mix well, and bring to a boil for 10 minutes. Drain the cooked shrimp in a colander and rinse with cold water for 5 minutes. Let stand to cool.

3. In a clean stockpot, make a brine by combining 1 gallon of water with 2 tablespoons of salt. Bring to a boil over high heat, stirring to dissolve the salt. If you are watching your salt intake, you may omit the salt and simply use boiling water. Once at a boil, remove from heat.

4. Peel the shrimp and pack into jars, leaving a 1-inch headspace. Ladle the brine over the shrimp. Remove any trapped air pockets and add additional brine if necessary to maintain the 1-inch headspace.

5. Wipe the jar rims with a washcloth dipped in vinegar. Place the lid and ring on each jar and hand tighten.

6. Process in a pressure canner at 10 PSI or according to your elevation and canner type. Process quart jars for 55 minutes; pint and half-pint jars both process for 45 minutes.

INGREDIENT TIP: *Retain shrimp peels in a plastic freezer bag and freeze immediately after peeling. The shells may be used to make home-canned shellfish stock.*

INGREDIENTS

11½ lbs. raw shrimp

2 gallons water, divided

1 cup white vinegar

½ cup + 2 T. canning and pickling salt, divided

Mexican Cuisine

Welcome to the vibrant and tantalizing world of Mexican cuisine! Bursting with rich flavors and vivid colors, Mexican food is a true celebration of culinary artistry. From the sizzling streets of Mexico City to the picturesque coastal towns, each region boasts its own unique culinary traditions and ingredients, offering a diverse tapestry of tastes and textures.

Mexico's culinary heritage is deeply rooted in its ancient civilizations, such as the Aztecs and Mayans, who cultivated corn, beans, and chili peppers as dietary staples. These foundational ingredients, combined with the introduction of livestock and culinary techniques brought by the Spanish conquistadors, form the backbone of Mexican cooking. Each dish in this chapter tells a story of the country's complex history and cultural fusion.

In this chapter, we'll explore the time-honored techniques, staple ingredients, and iconic dishes that have made Mexican food a beloved global phenomenon. Prepare to immerse yourself in a culture that cherishes food as an expression of joy, community, and tradition.

Mexican cuisine offers a variety of one-pot meals that are not only delicious but perfect for creating a meal in a jar. These dishes are often packed with authentic flavors, combining different ingredients and spices to create satisfying meals perfect for family gatherings, weeknight dinners, or any occasion when you want a satisfying and hassle-free meal. Recipes such as barbacoa, mole and pozoles, as well as hearty, filling soups will be featured in this chapter.

So, grab your apron, and prepare your taste buds for a fiesta of flavors. Let's get canning. *¡Buen provecho!*

Albondigas (Mexican Meatballs)

Brought to Mexico by the conquistadors, this authentic meatball soup is a staple in Mexican cuisine. This traditional soup is made with beef-and-herb meatballs in an aromatic tomato broth loaded with vegetables. There are many versions inspired by individual family favorites over the years, some made with potatoes and carrots, others with green beans and roasted tomatoes.

PREP TIME: 30 minutes   **COOK TIME:** 45 minutes
PROCESS TIME: 90 or 75 minutes   **YIELD:** 7 quarts or 14 pints

INGREDIENTS

2½ lbs. lean ground beef

⅓ cup maize or corn meal

1 small yellow onion, finely chopped (¼ cup)

12 garlic cloves, minced (2 T.)

½ tsp. salt (optional)

½ tsp. cracked black peppercorns

18 Roma tomatoes, cored and skin slit vertically on two sides (6 cups puree)

8 cups beef broth

8 cups water

6 medium russet potatoes, peeled and cubed (6 cups)

6 medium carrots, peeled and chopped (6 cups)

4 celery ribs, diced (1 cup)

1 T. coriander powder

1 T. azafran (safflower) petals

DIRECTIONS

1. Preheat the oven to 450°F (232°C) and place the rack in the top third of the oven. Line a rimmed baking sheet with aluminum foil or use an oven-safe baking rack inside the baking sheet.

2. In a large bowl, mix together the ground beef, maize, onion, garlic, salt (if using), and pepper. Form the meat mixture into 1-inch balls, yielding about 70 to 80 meatballs. Line the meatballs onto the baking sheet in a single layer and place it in the oven. Bake the meatballs for 10 minutes or until they are firm. Turn on the broiler and broil the meatballs for 5 minutes or until they are browned. Remove from heat and set them aside.

3. Line a separate rimmed cookie sheet with the tomatoes and place it under the broiler for 15 to 20 minutes or until the tomatoes are softened, turning the tomatoes once midway through broiling. Set the tomatoes aside to cool and then remove and discard any blackened skin. Process the roasted tomatoes in a food processor and empty it into a stockpot, or place the roasted tomatoes in a stockpot and puree them using a handheld stick emulsion blender.

> **Treat your glass jars like a glass coffee pot for years of continued use.**

4. Add the broth, water, potatoes, carrots, celery, coriander, and azafran to the tomato puree, mix well, and bring it to a boil over medium-high heat. Once the mixture is at a boil, add the meatballs to the stockpot and carefully stir to avoid breaking apart the meatballs. Cook for 10 minutes, then remove from heat.

5. Using a funnel and slotted spoon, evenly distribute the meatballs and vegetables into each jar leaving a generous 1¼-inch headspace. Ladle the soup base into each jar, leaving 1 inch of headspace. Remove any trapped air pockets and add additional soup base if necessary to maintain the 1-inch headspace.

6. Wipe the jar rims with a washcloth dipped in vinegar. Place the lid and ring on each jar and hand tighten.

7. Process in a pressure canner at 10 PSI or according to your elevation and canner type. Process quart jars for 90 minutes and pint jars for 75 minutes.

INGREDIENT TIP: *Azafran is a thistlelike petal from the safflower plant, a descendant from the sunflower family. It has an orange-red color known to give food an orange hue, amazing nutty aroma, and mild sweet flavoring.*

Beef Barbacoa

This is truly my family's favorite! I make this recipe about three times a year because we eat so much of it, I cannot keep it on my pantry shelf long enough. You may also make this recipe using pork, but we prefer beef. Having this recipe in your pantry makes mealtime quick and easy because you can make tacos or bean-and-rice bowls, you can stuff and bake flour tortillas to make enchiladas, or you can even use it as a salad topper. There's no wrong way to enjoy this versatile Mexican staple.

PREP TIME: 15 minutes   COOK TIME: 5 hours

PROCESS TIME: 90 or 75 minutes   YIELD: 5 quarts or 10 pints

DIRECTIONS

1. After cutting the beef into chunks, pat it dry with a paper towel and sprinkle the beef with salt and pepper. Heat the oil in a deep skillet over medium-high heat. Working in batches, add the beef to the stockpot and brown each side for 2 minutes, being careful not to over-crowd the stockpot. Once it is browned, place the beef at the bottom of your 8-quart Crock-Pot.

2. Using a food processor, puree the onion, peppers and adobo sauce, garlic, vinegar, lime juice, broth, cumin, and oregano. Empty the mixture into the Crock-Pot and add the bay leaves. Cook it for 5 hours on high.

3. Remove the bay leaves and discard. Using a fork in each hand, shred the beef and mix well with the sauce. Using a funnel and slotted spoon, add 3 cups of shredded beef to each quart jar and 1½ cups to each pint jar. Next, ladle the sauce over the meat, leaving 1 inch of headspace. Remove any trapped air pockets and add additional sauce if necessary to maintain the 1-inch headspace.

4. Wipe the jar rims with a washcloth dipped in vinegar. Place the lid and ring on each jar and hand tighten.

5. Process in a pressure canner at 10 PSI or according to your elevation and canner type. Process quart jars for 90 minutes and pint jars for 75 minutes.

INGREDIENTS

5 lbs. beef chuck roast, cut into 3-inch chunks

Salt and pepper, to taste

3 T. olive oil

1 large sweet onion, diced (2½ cups)

7 chipotle peppers in adobo sauce

1 head garlic, minced (¼ cup)

1 cup apple cider vinegar

½ cup lime juice

2 cups beef broth

3 T. cumin powder

2 T. dried oregano

2 bay leaves

Birria (Mexican Beef Stew)

Hailing from the state of Jalisco, this meat stew is commonly made with goat meat, mutton, or chicken, as well as beef. Heat a jar and serve in a bowl with your favorite toppings.

PREP TIME: 20 minutes   **COOK TIME:** 25 minutes
PROCESS TIME: 90 or 75 minutes   **YIELD:** 5 quarts or 10 pints

INGREDIENTS

- 4 dried ancho chilies, stems and seeds removed
- 4 dried guajillo chilies, stems and seeds removed
- 1 chipotle pepper, stems and seeds removed
- 5 lbs. beef chuck roast, cut into 2-inch chunks
- Salt and pepper, to taste
- 3 T. olive oil
- 5 cups beef stock, divided
- 6 Roma tomatoes, cored and diced (2 cups)
- 1 medium sweet onion, diced (1 cup)
- 12 garlic cloves, minced (2 T.)
- ½ cup apple cider vinegar
- 1 cup water
- 2 T. dried oregano
- 2 T. ground cumin
- 1 T. ground coriander
- 2 tsp. dried thyme
- 1 tsp. salt (optional)
- 1 tsp. marjoram
- 1 tsp. ground cinnamon
- ¼ tsp. ground clove

DIRECTIONS

1. In a heat-safe bowl, add the dried chilies and chipotle pepper and cover them with boiling water. Place a smaller bowl on top of the peppers to keep them submerged for 10 minutes.

2. After cutting the beef into chunks, pat it dry with a paper towel and sprinkle the beef with salt and pepper. Heat the oil in a deep skillet over medium-high heat. Working in batches, add the beef to the skillet and brown for 2 minutes on each side, being careful not to overcrowd the skillet. Set the browned beef aside.

3. Place the rehydrated chilies and the chipotle pepper into the food processor and discard the soaking water. Add 1 cup of the beef stock and all other remaining ingredients. Puree the mixture until it is smooth.

4. Empty the birria puree into a stockpot, add the remaining beef broth, and bring it to a boil over medium-high heat, stirring often. Carefully add the beef pieces to the stockpot, resting them on top of the sauce and not submerging them. Reduce the heat to simmer and braise the beef for 15 minutes.

5. Using tongs, fill each jar ¾ full with beef chunks, being sure to evenly distribute the meat, and leaving the top quarter of the jars empty. Using a funnel, ladle birria sauce into each jar, leaving 1 inch of headspace. Remove any trapped air pockets and add additional sauce if necessary to maintain the 1-inch headspace.

6. Wipe the jar rims with a washcloth dipped in vinegar. Place the lid and ring on each jar and hand tighten.

7. Process in a pressure canner at 10 PSI or according to your elevation and canner type. Process quart jars for 90 minutes and pint jars for 75 minutes.

Green Chili Verde with Pork

Green Chili Verde is my absolute favorite meal in a jar because it uses my salsa verde recipe combined with roasted poblano peppers and tender pork medallions, creating an amazing stew. It is truly so flavorful and boasts a beautiful green hue. Serve with warm tortillas, rice, and beans for a remarkable meal in minutes.

PREP TIME: 20 minutes   **COOK TIME: 40 minutes**
PROCESS TIME: 90 or 75 minutes   **YIELD: 5 quarts or 10 pints**

DIRECTIONS

1. Preheat the oven to 450°F (232°C). Using a rimmed baking sheet, place the tomatillos flesh-side down onto the sheet and roast them for 20 minutes or until the tomatillos are lightly charred and soft. Remove the sheet from the oven and let the tomatillos cool.

2. Heat 1 tablespoon of the oil in a large stockpot over medium-high heat. Working in batches, add the pork to the stockpot and brown each side for 2 to 3 minutes, being careful not to overcrowd the stockpot. Remove from heat and set aside.

3. Using a food processor, puree the onions, jalapeños, and garlic. Empty the mixture into the same stockpot used to brown the pork. Working in batches, puree the cooled roasted tomatillos and their juice and add the puree to the stock pot. Add the lime juice, cumin, paprika, salt, cilantro, and browned pork and mix well. Bring it to a boil, and allow the mixture to boil for 5 minutes, stirring often. Remove from heat.

4. Using a funnel and slotted spoon, evenly distribute the pork among the jars. Next, ladle the verde sauce into each jar, leaving 1 inch of headspace. Remove any trapped air pockets and add additional verde sauce if necessary to maintain the 1-inch headspace.

5. Wipe the jar rims with a washcloth dipped in vinegar. Place the lid and ring on each jar and hand tighten.

6. Process in a pressure canner at 10 PSI or according to your elevation and canner type. Process quart jars for 90 minutes and pint jars for 75 minutes.

INGREDIENTS

32 tomatillos (6 lbs.), husks removed and halved

4 T. vegetable oil, divided

9 lbs. pork loin, or pork shoulder, trimmed and cut into 1-inch pieces (10 cups)

2 white onions, chopped (3 cups)

2 to 4 jalapeños, stems and seeds removed, finely chopped (1 to 2 cups)

12 garlic cloves, minced (2 T.)

1 cup fresh lime juice

1 T. ground cumin

2 tsp. smoked paprika

2 tsp. salt

½ cup coarsely chopped fresh cilantro

Chile Rellenos

Enjoy this fun spin on a Mexican favorite using poblano peppers, corn, black beans, tomatoes, and seasonings. When you're ready to eat it, carefully remove the stuffed peppers from their wide-mouthed jar, place them onto a baking dish cut-side up, sprinkle with cheese, and bake them at 400°F (204°C) for 20 to 25 minutes or until they are cooked through and bubbling.

PREP TIME: 15 minutes   COOK TIME: 50 minutes
PROCESS TIME: 90 minutes   YIELD: 7 quarts

INGREDIENTS

- 21 poblano peppers with stems intact
- 3 (15 oz.) cans black beans, drained and rinsed
- 10 Roma tomatoes, diced (3½ cups)
- 2½ cups corn kernels, fresh or frozen
- 1 Spanish onion, diced (2 cups)
- 2 jalapeños, stems and seeds removed and diced (1 cup)
- 1 bunch cilantro, chopped (1 cup)
- 1 head garlic, peeled and minced (¼ cup)
- 2 T. chili powder
- 2 tsp. garlic powder
- 2 tsp. onion powder
- 2 tsp. dried oregano
- 2 tsp. paprika
- 1 tsp. ground cumin
- 1 tsp. salt
- 1 tsp. ground black pepper
- 1 (6 oz.) can tomato paste
- ½ cup water

DIRECTIONS

1. Preheat the oven to 450°F (232°C). Line a baking sheet with parchment paper and place the whole poblano peppers on the paper. Roast them for 20 to 25 minutes, turning the peppers once halfway through. Remove them from the oven to cool after both sides have blistered but not burned.

2. In a large stockpot, place the black beans, tomatoes, corn, onion, jalapeño, cilantro, and garlic. Mix well and bring it to a boil over medium-high heat. Stirring often, boil the mixture for 5 minutes, then reduce the heat and simmer for 15 minutes. Add the chili powder, garlic powder, onion powder, oregano, paprika, cumin, salt, and pepper, and mix well to blend in the spices. Add the tomato paste and water and stir until the tomato is fully dispersed. Continue to simmer for 5 minutes or until the filling has thickened.

3. Place the poblano peppers on a cutting board. Using a paring knife, gently cut longways through one side of the pepper to create a pocket. Remove and discard the seeds and membrane from inside the pepper. Using a tablespoon, fill the pocket with a generous ½ cup of the filling.

4. Carefully slide 3 stuffed peppers into each wide-mouthed quart jar, being sure the stem is below the ½-inch headspace mark.

5. Wipe the jar rims with a washcloth dipped in vinegar. Place the lid and ring on each jar and hand tighten.

6. Process in a pressure canner at 10 PSI or according to your elevation and canner type. Process quart jars for 90 minutes.

RECIPE TIP: *When filling the wide-mouthed jars with stuffed poblano peppers, have the cut side face the outside of the jar to help keep the filling inside the pepper during processing. While this recipe is best suited for wide-mouthed quart jars, if your stuffed peppers are small enough to fit in a wide-mouthed pint jar, process the pint jars for 75 minutes according to your elevation.*

Margarita Chicken

Inspired by Mexican flavors and the popular margarita cocktail, this recipe incorporates fresh lime and orange juice, cherry tomatoes, fresh herbs, and tequila for a colorful fiesta in a jar. Enjoy this delicious chicken dish topped with freshly sliced avocado, chopped cilantro, and a lime wedge.

PREP TIME: 20 minutes   COOK TIME: 25 minutes
PROCESS TIME: 90 or 75 minutes   YIELD: 5 quarts or 10 pints

INGREDIENTS

2 cups tequila

2 cups orange juice

1 cup lime juice

½ cup agave sweetener

5½ lbs. boneless, skinless chicken breasts (10½ cups)

2 cups chicken broth

36 oz. cherry tomatoes, halved (4 cups)

3 red bell peppers, chopped (3 cups)

2 green bell peppers, chopped (2 cups)

1 red onion, diced (2½ cups)

2 jalapeños, diced (1 cup)

1 head garlic, peeled and minced (¼ cup)

1 bunch fresh cilantro, chopped (1 cup)

2 T. cumin

1 T. dried oregano

1 T. ground coriander

2 tsp. salt (optional)

1 tsp. ground black pepper

DIRECTIONS

1. Place the tequila, orange juice, lime juice, and agave in a stockpot and mix well. Layer the chicken breasts into the liquid, submerging as much of the chicken as possible. Over medium-high heat, bring it to a boil, then reduce the heat and simmer for 15 minutes or until the chicken is fully cooked. Using tongs, remove the chicken breasts to cool on a cutting board.

2. Add the broth, tomatoes, red and green peppers, red onion, jalapeños, and garlic to the stockpot, mix well, and bring it to a boil. Chop the chicken into 1-inch pieces and add them to the stockpot along with the cilantro, cumin, oregano, coriander, salt, and pepper. Mix well and return the mixture to a boil for 5 minutes.

3. Using a funnel and slotted spoon, evenly distribute the chicken mixture into each jar, leaving a generous 1¼-inch of head space. Next, ladle the broth into each jar, leaving the generous 1-inch headspace. Remove any trapped air pockets and add additional broth if necessary to maintain the generous 1-inch headspace.

4. Wipe the jar rims with a washcloth dipped in vinegar. Place the lid and ring on each jar and hand tighten.

5. Process in a pressure canner at 10 PSI or according to your elevation and canner type. Process quart jars for 90 minutes and pint jars for 75 minutes.

Mexican Bean Soup

Filled to the brim with beans and vegetables, this authentically spiced soup is warm and inviting. Known as sopa de frijoles in Spanish, it has evolved over time yet remains a popular and cherished dish in Mexican cuisine. Serve it with diced avocado, chopped cilantro, and tortilla strips.

PREP TIME: 60 minutes **COOK TIME:** 35 minutes
PROCESS TIME: 90 or 75 minutes **YIELD:** 5 quarts or 10 pints

INGREDIENTS

- 1½ cups dried pinto beans or 3 (15 oz.) cans pinto beans
- 1 cup dried kidney beans or 2 (15 oz.) cans kidney beans
- 3 lbs. ground Mexican chorizo (4½ cups)
- 1 large sweet onion, diced (3 cups)
- 1 head garlic, peeled and minced (¼ cup)
- 12 Roma tomatoes, chopped (4 cups)
- 2 cups corn kernels, fresh or frozen
- 1 red bell pepper, diced (1 cup)
- 1 (6 oz.) can tomato paste
- 2 T. ground cumin
- 1 T. dried oregano
- 1 T. paprika
- 2 tsp. salt (optional)
- 1 tsp. ground black pepper
- 8 cups chicken broth

DIRECTIONS

1. Thoroughly rinse the dried beans in a colander, being sure to remove any rocks, debris, or disfigured beans. Place the beans in a stockpot and cover them with water. Bring it to a boil over high heat, and allow the beans to boil for 10 minutes. Remove from heat, cover the stockpot, and steep the beans for 1 hour.

2. Place the chorizo in a separate stockpot and cook it over medium-high heat, breaking the meat apart into small pieces with a spatula. After 5 minutes, add the onion and garlic, mix well, and continue to cook them for about 10 minutes or until the onion is soft.

3. Empty the beans in a colander in the sink and rinse them. Add the beans, tomatoes, corn, peppers, tomato paste, cumin, oregano, paprika, salt, and pepper to the stockpot. Mix well. Cook for 5 minutes, stirring often, then slowly add the broth, scraping any bits from the bottom of the pot. Bring it to a boil, and allow the soup to boil for 5 minutes, stirring often.

4. Using a funnel, ladle the soup into each jar, leaving 1 inch of headspace. Remove any trapped air pockets and add additional soup if necessary to maintain the 1-inch headspace.

5. Wipe the jar rims with a washcloth dipped in vinegar. Place the lid and ring on each jar and hand tighten.

6. Process in a pressure canner at 10 PSI or according to your elevation and canner type. Process quart jars for 90 minutes and pint jars for 75 minutes.

RECIPE TIP: *As the jars cool after processing, the soup will naturally become thicker and may soak up a good portion of the liquid. Upon reheating, the soup will reconstitute; however, you may add additional broth to the pan.*

Spicy Beef Fajitas

While most of us think of fajitas as freshly grilled, this recipe provides a delicious way to preserve them in a jar to later heat and serve wrapped in warm tortillas. Feel free to create the spice level to your liking, scaling it on the milder side or making the beef superhot.

PREP TIME: 20 minutes **COOK TIME:** 10 minutes
PROCESS TIME: 90 or 75 minutes **YIELD:** 5 quarts or 10 pints

DIRECTIONS

1. Thoroughly rinse the dried beans in a colander, being sure to remove any rocks, debris, or disfigured beans. Place the beans in a stockpot and cover them with water. Using your hands, agitate the beans in the water to remove any dirt. Empty the beans into the colander and rinse them again. Using wide-mouthed jars, add ½ cup of beans to each quart jar and ¼ cup to each pint jar. Set the jars aside.

2. Heat 1 tablespoon of the oil in a deep skillet over high heat. Working in batches, add the steak to the skillet and quickly sear each side for 15 seconds, then remove it from the skillet. Add 1 cup of the seared beef to each quart jar and ½ cup to each pint jar.

3. Next add 1 cup of peppers to each quart and ½ cup to each pint. Continue with the onions, adding ½ cup to each quart and ¼ cup to each pint. Add 1 tablespoon of lime juice, 1 tablespoon of soy sauce, and 1 tablespoon of garlic powder to each quart jar and ½ tablespoon of each to every pint jar. Add 1 teaspoon of cumin, 1 teaspoon of chili powder and 1 teaspoon of oregano to each quart jar and ½ teaspoon of each to every pint jar.

4. Using a funnel, slowly ladle the beef broth into every jar, leaving 1 inch of headspace. Remove any trapped air pockets and add additional broth if necessary to maintain the 1-inch headspace.

5. Wipe the jar rims with a washcloth dipped in vinegar. Place the lid and ring on each jar and hand tighten.

6. Process in a pressure canner at 10 PSI or according to your elevation and canner type. Process quart jars for 90 minutes and pint jars for 75 minutes.

INGREDIENTS

3 cups dried pinto beans

2 T. vegetable oil, divided

6 lbs. skirt steak or flank steak, sliced ½-inch thick against grain (5 cups)

5 bell peppers (any color combination), sliced (5 cups)

2 large sweet onions, sliced (2½ cups)

5 T. lime juice

5 T. soy sauce

5 T. garlic powder

5 tsp. ground cumin

5 tsp. chili powder

5 tsp. dried oregano

8 cups beef broth

Pork Posole

Loaded with cubed pork, Mexican chorizo, hominy, and an array of spices, this classic is truly a blessing in a jar. Simply empty a jar into a saucepan, heat it, and eat. Want to showcase your posole for company? Serve it alongside freshly baked Mexican corn bread and a side of black beans and rice.

PREP TIME: 20 minutes   COOK TIME: 30 minutes
PROCESS TIME: 90 or 75 minutes   YIELD: 7 quarts or 14 pints

DIRECTIONS

1. Place the oil in a stockpot and heat it over medium-high heat. Add the pork and allow it to cook on one side for 3 minutes without disturbing it. Remove from heat and set it aside. In the same stockpot, add the chorizo and cook it for about 10 minutes or until it is cooked through, using a spatula to separate the meat into smaller pieces as it cooks. Return the pork to the stockpot and mix well.

2. Add the stock, hominy, tomatoes, onion, corn, jalapeño, garlic, chili powder, coriander, cumin, salt (if using), and pepper to the stockpot and mix well. Bring it to a boil, then reduce the heat and simmer the posole for 15 minutes, stirring often.

3. Using a funnel, ladle the posole into jars, leaving a 1-inch headspace. Remove any trapped air pockets and add additional posole if necessary to maintain the 1-inch headspace.

4. Wipe the jar rims with a washcloth dipped in vinegar. Place the lid and ring on each jar and hand tighten.

5. Process in a pressure canner at 10 PSI or according to your elevation and canner type. Process quart jars for 90 minutes and pint jars for 75 minutes.

INGREDIENTS

2 T. vegetable oil

1½ lbs. boneless pork shoulder, cubed (5 cups)

1 lb. ground Mexican chorizo

8 cups chicken stock

2 (16 oz.) cans hominy, drained (5 cups)

9 Roma tomatoes, chopped (3 cups)

1 large sweet onion, diced (3 cups)

2 cups corn kernels, fresh or frozen

3 jalapeños, diced (1½ cups)

1 head garlic, peeled and minced (¼ cup)

¼ cup chili powder

2 T. ground coriander

1 T. ground cumin

2 tsp. salt (optional)

1 tsp. ground black pepper

Mole Poblano

The exact origin of mole is still a subject of debate, but indigenous civilizations in Mexico, such as the Aztecs and the Zapotecs, had a long-standing tradition of creating complex sauces using a wide range of ingredients. The most famous and widely recognized version of the sauce is mole poblano, and it is traditionally served over turkey or chicken. It is a staple dish during special occasions and holidays like Day of the Dead and Christmas. Making and preserving this extensive and intricate mole will save you hours in meal preparation. Simply fry your chicken, heat your mole, and serve.

**PREP TIME: 60 minutes COOK TIME: 50 minutes
PROCESS TIME: 75 or 60 minutes YIELD: 4 quarts, or 8 pints, or 16 half pints**

INGREDIENTS

- 12 dried ancho chilies, stems and seeds removed
- 12 dried guajillo or mulato chilies, stems and seeds removed
- 12 dried pasilla chilies, stems and seeds removed
- ½ cup sesame seeds
- 2 tsp. aniseed
- 2 tsp. coriander seeds
- 2 tsp. black peppercorns
- 1 tsp. whole cloves
- 5 dried bay leaves, crumbled
- 2 sticks cinnamon, broken into pieces
- 3 T. vegetable oil
- 1½ cups skin-on almonds
- 1 cup hulled pumpkin seeds (pepitas)
- ½ cup unsalted peanuts
- 1 cup raisins
- 4 large tomatoes, cored and quartered (4 cups)
- 2 medium onions, diced (2 cups)
- 1 head garlic, minced (¼ cup)
- 16 cups chicken stock, divided
- 1 tsp. salt (optional)
- 2 cups Mexican chocolate, chopped

DIRECTIONS

1. Place the dried chilies in a heat-safe bowl and cover with boiling water. Place a smaller bowl on top of the chilies to keep them submerged for 30 minutes. After the chilies are rehydrated, reserve 1 cup of the soaking water.

2. Working in batches, add a third of the chilies and ⅓ cup of the soaking water to a food processor and puree until the mixture is smooth. Empty the puree into a bowl and set it aside as you puree the next two batches.

3. Using a spice grinder or food processor, add the sesame seeds, aniseed, coriander seeds, peppercorns, cloves, bay leaves, and cinnamon and process until they are finely ground. Set the mixture aside.

4. In a large skillet on medium-high heat, place the oil, almonds, pumpkin seeds, peanuts, and raisins. Toss and heat the ingredients for about five minutes or until the raisins are plump and the nuts are slightly browned. Remove them from the skillet with slotted spoon, or sieve, and rest them in a bowl.

5. In the same skillet, heat the oil remaining in the pan and cook the tomatoes, onions, and garlic for about 10 minutes or until the tomatoes and onions are browned. Remove from heat and set it aside to cool.

Never start your timer before the stovetop pressure canner reaches the required PSI.

6. In a stockpot, or Dutch oven, place the chili puree, 4 cups of stock, and the salt (if using). Mix well and bring the stock to a boil over medium-high heat. Reduce the heat to simmer and add the ground spices, mixing well.

7. Place the tomato mixture, the toasted nuts and raisins, and 4 cups of stock in a food processor and puree until smooth, then add it to the stockpot, mixing well. Add the remaining stock and return it to a simmer. Add the chocolate and simmer for 30 minutes, stirring often.

8. Using a funnel, ladle the mole into jars, leaving a 1-inch headspace. Remove any trapped air pockets and add additional mole if necessary to maintain the 1-inch headspace.

9. Wipe the jar rims with a washcloth dipped in vinegar. Place the lid and ring on each jar and hand tighten.

10. Process in a pressure canner at 10 PSI or according to your elevation and canner type. Process quart jars for 75 minutes and pint and half-pint jars for 60 minutes.

Taco Soup

My kids and I love this recipe! While tacos are delicious in a hard or soft shell, there is something to be said about enjoying its many flavors in a hearty soup made from traditional ingredients like ground beef, tomatoes, corn, and beans. Your family will insist on having a generous supply on your pantry shelf every year. I personally prefer canning this in pints as it is a perfect single-portion meal.

PREP TIME: **10 minutes**   COOK TIME: **30 minutes**
PROCESS TIME: **90 or 75 minutes**   YIELD: **9 quarts or 18 pints**

INGREDIENTS

4 lbs. ground beef

3 T. dried oregano

1 sweet onion, diced (2 cups)

1 medium green bell pepper, chopped (1 cup)

2 jalapeños, finely chopped (½ cup)

12 garlic cloves, minced (2 T.)

24 Roma tomatoes, diced (8 cups)

1 (8 oz.) can diced green chilies

8 cups beef broth

2 cups water

3 cups corn kernels, fresh or frozen

1 (15 oz.) can pinto beans

1 (15 oz.) can black beans

1 bunch cilantro, chopped (1 cup)

¼ cup chili powder

⅛ cup cumin powder

DIRECTIONS

1. In a large stockpot over medium-high heat, brown the ground beef and oregano for about 15 minutes or until it is fully cooked. Remove any excess grease. Stir in the onion, peppers, jalapeños, garlic, tomatoes, and chilies and cook for an additional 10 minutes. Stir often to avoid scorching the tomatoes.

2. Add the remaining ingredients to the stockpot and mix well. Bring it to a boil, and allow the soup to boil for 5 minutes, stirring often to avoid scorching.

3. Using a funnel, ladle soup into jars, leaving a 1-inch headspace.

4. Wipe the jar rims with a washcloth dipped in vinegar. Place the lid and ring on each jar and hand tighten.

5. Process in a pressure canner at 10 PSI or according to your elevation and canner type. Process quart jars for 90 minutes and pint jars for 75 minutes.

INGREDIENT TIP: *If you prefer to use dried beans versus canned beans, fully rehydrate ½ cup of each bean by soaking them for a minimum of 4 hours prior to rinsing and using them in this recipe. The overall acidity of the ingredients makes it harder for the beans to soften during processing, so I purposely use home-canned or store-bought beans.*

Zucchini Chicken Dinner

Zucchini is a popular vegetable used in Mexican soups and meals with protein. Combining zucchini and chicken with sweet potatoes and carrots, this simple, healthy meal is the perfect solution for a busy night without much time to cook from scratch. Heat a jar's worth on the stovetop and serve alongside steamed rice and warm tortillas.

PREP TIME: 30 minutes   **COOK TIME:** 15 minutes
PROCESS TIME: 90 or 75 minutes   **YIELD:** 7 quarts or 14 pints

DIRECTIONS

1. Place the oil and chicken in a skillet and cook the meat over medium-high heat for 5 minutes on each side. Remove the chicken from the skillet to cool on a cutting board. Once cooled, cut it into bite-size cubes and set the chicken aside. Work in batches if needed.

2. Place the cubed chicken in a large stockpot and add all remaining ingredients. Cook over medium-high heat for 5 minutes, stirring often to blend ingredients.

3. Using a funnel, ladle the mixture into jars, leaving a 1-inch headspace. Remove any trapped air pockets and add additional mixture if necessary to maintain the 1-inch headspace.

4. Wipe the jar rims with a washcloth dipped in vinegar. Place the lid and ring on each jar and hand tighten.

5. Process in a pressure canner at 10 PSI or according to your elevation and canner type. Process quart jars for 90 minutes and pint jars for 75 minutes.

INGREDIENT TIP: *If you would prefer to use beans for protein instead of chicken, simply rehydrate 2½ cups of pinto beans by soaking them in water for 4 hours, then rinse and add to the recipe. If you prefer store-bought or home-canned beans, use 4 (15 oz.) cans (or pint jars) of pinto beans.*

INGREDIENTS

3 T. vegetable oil

3 lbs. boneless, skinless chicken breasts (6 cups)

1 lb. boneless, skinless chicken thighs (2 cups)

6 zucchinis, cubed (9 cups)

12 Roma tomatoes, diced (4 cups)

3 medium sweet potatoes, peeled and cubed (3 cups)

2 medium green bell peppers, diced (2 cups)

3 medium carrots, peeled and diced (1½ cups)

1 yellow onion, diced (1½ cups)

12 garlic cloves, minced (2 T.)

2 T. ground coriander

1 T. cumin

1 to 2 tsp. ground cayenne pepper (optional)

Spicy Chicken with Canary Beans

The Peruano bean is common in Mexico and has been cultivated for centuries. Named for its beautiful yellow color resembling the feathers of a canary, the Peruvian bean has a delicate nutty taste and mild, buttery flavor. Enjoy this authentic meal in a jar with steamed rice, sliced avocado, and chopped cilantro.

PREP TIME: 70 minutes   COOK TIME: 50 minutes
PROCESS TIME: 90 or 75 minutes   YIELD: 7 quarts or 14 pints

INGREDIENTS

3 cups dried canary beans

1 lb. thick-cut bacon, cut into 1-inch pieces

5½ lbs. boneless, skinless chicken breasts (10½ cups)

3 medium green bell peppers, diced (3 cups)

1 yellow onion, diced (1½ cups)

1 head garlic, peeled and minced (¼ cup)

8 cups chicken stock

6 cups water

1 (6 oz.) can tomato paste

½ cup *aji panca* chili paste

¼ cup honey

¼ cup red wine vinegar

2 T. lime juice

1 T. dried oregano

1 T. ground cumin

DIRECTIONS

1. Thoroughly rinse the dried beans in a colander, being sure to remove any rocks, debris, or disfigured beans. Place the beans in a stockpot and cover them with water. Bring it to a boil over high heat, and allow the beans to boil for 10 minutes. Remove from heat, cover the stockpot, and steep the beans for 1 hour.

2. Add the bacon to a stockpot over medium-high heat and fry it for about 8 minutes or until the bacon is crisp but not burnt. Remove bacon from the stockpot to cool. In the same stockpot, add the chicken thighs and brown them on each side for 5 minutes. Remove to cool. Once cool to touch, cut chicken into bite-size pieces.

3. Empty the steeped beans into a colander in the sink and rinse. Add the bacon, chicken, peppers, onion, and garlic to the stockpot and mix well. Cook for 5 minutes. Slowly add 1 cup of the stock and deglaze the pan. Add the remaining stock, water, tomato paste, *aji panca* paste, honey, vinegar, lime juice, oregano, cumin, and beans. Mix well. Bring it to a boil, then reduce the heat and simmer for 25 minutes, stirring often.

> **Storing your home-canned goods out of direct or indirect sunlight will help increase their shelf life.**

4. Using a funnel, ladle the mixture into jars, leaving a 1-inch headspace. Remove any trapped air pockets and add additional mixture if necessary to maintain the 1-inch headspace.

5. Wipe the jar rims with a washcloth dipped in vinegar. Place the lid and ring on each jar and hand tighten.

6. Process in a pressure canner at 10 PSI or according to your elevation and canner type. Process quart jars for 90 minutes and pint jars for 75 minutes.

INGREDIENT TIP: *Most Mexican supply stores carry yellow* Peruano (canary) *beans. If you are unable to find* Peruano *beans, not to worry. Feel free to substitute pinto beans for a delicious outcome.*

American and European Cuisine

European cuisine underwent significant changes from the Middle Ages to the Renaissance period. Spices played a prominent role in adding flavor to dishes, with trade routes bringing exotic spices from Asia to Europe and the rise of the wealthy merchant class making dining a lavish affair. The Age of Exploration expanded European cuisine, thanks to explorers and traders who ventured into new lands and brought back exotic ingredients like potatoes, tomatoes, chocolate, and spices, which revolutionized European cooking. This culinary exchange led to a fusion of flavors and techniques, creating new and exciting dishes across the continent.

The birth of American cuisine is deeply intertwined with the culinary evolution of our European predecessors. As Europeans began exploring and settling in the Americas, they brought with them their culinary traditions, ingredients, and cooking techniques, introducing European flavors to the New World, which laid the foundation for what would eventually become American cuisine.

Over time, as more immigrants from different European countries arrived in America, a true melting pot of culinary influences emerged. Immigrants from England, Germany, Ireland, Italy, France, and other European nations all contributed to the diversity that defines American cuisine.

This chapter includes a variety of recipes you may preserve and store on your pantry shelf. From the bold and robust tastes of American comfort food to the delicate and intricate flavors of European classics, every home canner will enjoy a delicious sampling of flavors, cultures, and traditions.

Bangers and Mash

The ultimate comfort food of Britain and Ireland, this delicious meal in a jar boasts meat sausages, known as "bangers," and potatoes, known as "mash," which are then slathered and processed in a rich onion gravy. I particularly enjoy heating a jarful on those cold, wet days of spring or fall. After heating the meal, simply mash the potatoes with a fork and serve it with a side of green peas.

PREP TIME: 20 minutes **COOK TIME:** 65 minutes
PROCESS TIME: 90 minutes **YIELD:** 7 quarts

INGREDIENTS

2 T. olive oil

21 (4 to 5-inch) pork sausage links or bratwursts, no longer than 5 inches each

8 lbs. yellow potatoes, peeled and quartered (14 cups)

8 T. (1 stick) butter

6 large yellow onions, peeled and sliced (9 cups)

1 T. dark brown sugar

1½ cups red wine (cabernet, merlot, or pinot noir)

6 cups beef stock

1 T. Worcestershire sauce

1 tsp. black pepper

¼ cup ClearJel

½ cup water

DIRECTIONS

1. Heat the oil in a skillet over medium-high heat. Working in batches, add the sausage to the skillet and brown each side for about 2 minutes, being careful not to overcrowd the skillet. Remove and set aside to cool.

2. Pack 3 links into a wide-mouthed glass jar by tipping the jar on its side and laying the links on top of one another. Next, raw pack the potato quarters in the remaining space, leaving 1 inch of headspace. Stand the packed jars upright onto a cutting board.

3. In a thick bottomed pot, melt the butter over medium-high heat. Add the onion and cook for 10 minutes, stirring occasionally but allowing the onion to sweat. Sprinkle the sugar over the onion and continue to cook, stirring occasionally, for 30 minutes or until the onion has caramelized. Slowly add the red wine and bring it to a rapid boil. Add the stock, Worcestershire sauce, and black pepper to the pot, mix well, and return it to a rapid boil. Reduce the heat and simmer for 15 minutes.

4. In a small bowl, mix the ClearJel and water together to create a slurry, then add it to the pot. Mix well to fully disperse the ClearJel, then remove from heat.

5. Using a funnel, ladle the gravy into each jar, being sure the sauce surrounds the links and potatoes. Leave a 1-inch headspace. Remove any trapped air pockets and add additional gravy if necessary to maintain the 1-inch headspace.

6. Wipe the jar rims with a washcloth dipped in vinegar. Place the lid and ring on each jar and hand tighten.

7. Process in a pressure canner at 10 PSI or according to your elevation and canner type. Process quart jars for 90 minutes.

INGREDIENT TIP: *If you do not eat pork, you may substitute beef or chicken sausages for this recipe. No matter the choice of meat, the delicious onion gravy will complement it beautifully.*

BBQ Country-Style Pork Ribs

This delicious recipe is a must-have in your pantry! The amazing BBQ sauce and tender meat makes for a meal that is finger-licking good. Take a jar camping or pull a jar from the pantry when you need dinner on the table in minutes. Simply heat through in a saucepan and serve alongside an ear of corn and your favorite potato salad.

PREP TIME: 5 minutes   **COOK TIME: 10 minutes**
PROCESS TIME: 90 or 75 minutes   **YIELD: 5 quarts or 10 pints**

INGREDIENTS

2 T. olive oil

8 lbs. pork butt country-style pork ribs, deboned

6 cups tomato sauce

6 cups ketchup

1 cup maple syrup

½ cup light brown sugar, packed

¾ cup molasses

¾ cup apple cider vinegar

½ cup Worcestershire sauce

1 head garlic, peeled and minced (¼ cup)

⅓ cup chili powder

4 T. paprika

4 T. onion powder

1 T. black pepper

1 T. salt (optional)

DIRECTIONS

1. Heat the oil in a deep skillet over high heat. Working in batches, add the ribs and sear each side for 30 seconds. Tightly raw pack 4 to 5 ribs per wide-mouthed quart jar or 2 to 3 ribs per wide-mouthed pint jar, leaving 1 inch of headspace.

2. Place all remaining ingredients in a stockpot, whisk them together, and cook over medium heat for about 5 minutes. Continue to whisk the sauce as it cooks, to blend the flavors and heat it through.

3. Using a funnel, ladle BBQ sauce into each jar, leaving 1 inch of headspace. Remove any trapped air pockets and add additional sauce if necessary to maintain the 1-inch headspace.

4. Wipe the jar rims with a washcloth dipped in vinegar. Place the lid and ring on each jar and hand tighten.

5. Process in a pressure canner at 10 PSI or according to your elevation and canner type. Process quart jars for 90 minutes and pint jars for 75 minutes.

INGREDIENT TIP: *If you wish for your BBQ sauce to have a smoky flavor, you may add ½ cup to ¾ cup of liquid smoke to the recipe when creating the BBQ sauce.*

Beef Paprikash

This hearty, delicious recipe stems from Hungarian goulash but has been Americanized and is made without added vegetables. Once a jar is reheated, feel free to thicken the sauce with flour or ClearJel. Add a spoonful of sour cream to each bowl or serve it over a baked potato and sprinkle it with chopped chives.

PREP TIME: 10 minutes   COOK TIME: 40 minutes
PROCESS TIME: 90 or 75 minutes   YIELD: 7 quarts or 14 pints

DIRECTIONS

1. Heat the oil in a stockpot and over medium-high heat. Working in batches, quickly brown the beef on all sides, about 5 minutes per batch, being careful not to overcrowd the stockpot or cook the beef all the way through. Set the beef aside.

2. Add the onion, garlic, caraway, marjoram, salt (if using), and pepper to the stockpot, mix well, and cook for about 10 minutes or until the onion is translucent. Slowly add ½ cup of the wine, scraping the bottom of the pan to remove all the bits and deglaze it. Allow the wine to cook down for 5 minutes undisturbed. Add the remaining wine and the peppers, broth, paprika, tomato paste, brown sugar, and browned beef and mix well. Cook the mixture for 15 minutes, stirring often.

3. Using a funnel, ladle the mixture into jars, leaving a 1-inch headspace. Remove any trapped air pockets and add additional mixture if necessary to maintain the 1-inch headspace.

4. Wipe the jar rims with a washcloth dipped in vinegar. Place the lid and ring on each jar and hand tighten.

5. Process in a pressure canner at 10 PSI or according to your elevation and canner type. Process quart jars for 90 minutes and pint jars for 75 minutes.

INGREDIENTS

3 T. olive oil

6 lbs. stewing beef

2 large onions, diced (3 cups)

1 head garlic, peeled and minced (¼ cup)

2 T. caraway seeds

2 tsp. marjoram

2 tsp. salt (optional)

1 tsp. black pepper

1 cup red wine (cabernet or merlot), divided

7 red bell peppers, chopped (7 cups)

8 cups beef broth

½ cup paprika

1 (6 oz.) can tomato paste

1 T. brown sugar

Beef Pot Pie Filling

This recipe boasts deep, rich flavors and is the perfect addition to your pantry. Feel free to make this recipe using venison, bison, or elk meat. The ultimate comfort food, this hearty recipe may be made into a pot pie or heated in a saucepan and served over mashed potatoes, or used for individual pies baked in ramekins.

PREP TIME: 25 minutes   **COOK TIME:** 40 minutes
PROCESS TIME: 90 or 75 minutes   **YIELD:** 8 quarts or 16 pints

INGREDIENTS

3 T. olive oil

3 lbs. beef chuck roast, cut into 1-inch pieces

8 oz. white button mushrooms, chopped (3 cups)

1 large onion, diced (1½ cups)

1 head garlic, peeled and smashed (½ cup)

1 cup red wine (cabernet)

6 carrots, peeled and diced (3 cups)

2 russet potatoes, peeled and diced (2 cups)

2 cups peas (fresh or frozen)

3 Roma tomatoes, diced (1 cup)

1 (6 oz.) can tomato paste

8 cups beef broth

3 T. Worcestershire sauce

6 sprigs fresh thyme or 2 tsp. dried thyme

2 bay leaves

2 tsp. black pepper

1 tsp. salt (optional)

1 cup ClearJel

1 cup water

DIRECTIONS

1. Heat the oil in a stockpot over medium-high heat. Working in batches, quickly brown the beef on all sides, about 5 minutes per batch, being careful not to overcrowd the beef or cook it all the way through. Set the beef aside.

2. Add the mushrooms, onion, and garlic to the stockpot, mix well, and cook for about 5 minutes or until the onion is translucent. Slowly add the wine, scraping the bottom of the pan to remove all the bits and deglaze the pan. Allow the wine to cook down for 5 minutes undisturbed. Add the carrots, potatoes, peas, tomatoes, and paste, mix well, and cook the mixture for an additional 5 minutes, stirring often. Next, add the beef broth, Worcestershire, thyme, bay leaves, salt, pepper, and browned beef and mix well. Bring it to a boil, then reduce the heat and simmer for 15 minutes, stirring occasionally. Remove and discard the thyme sprigs and bay leaves.

3. In a small bowl, whisk the ClearJel and water together to create a slurry. Slowly add it to the stockpot and mix well to disperse the ClearJel, then remove the pot from heat. The filling will start to thicken. (If the filling begins to get too thick while cooking, add water in ½ cup increments to achieve the desired consistency.)

4. Using a funnel, ladle the filling into each jar, leaving a 1-inch headspace. Remove any trapped air pockets and add additional filling if necessary to maintain the 1-inch headspace.

5. Wipe the jar rims with a washcloth dipped in vinegar. Place the lid and ring on each jar and hand tighten.

6. Process in a pressure canner at 10 PSI or according to your elevation and canner type. Process quart jars for 90 minutes and pint jars for 75 minutes.

French Onion Soup

Originating in Paris, France, it has been told the soup was invented by King Louis XV in his hunting lodge. It started with onions, butter, and champagne because these were the only ingredients he had on hand at the time. Today, this soup is a national treasure. Enjoy it baked in a crock bowl topped with grated Gruyère cheese and toasted bread.

PREP TIME: 20 minutes   **COOK TIME:** 50 minutes
PROCESS TIME: 75 or 60 minutes   **YIELD:** 5 quarts or 10 pints

DIRECTIONS

1. In a large stockpot, melt the butter over medium heat. Add the sweet and red onions and the garlic to the stockpot and mix to coat. Reduce the heat to low and allow the onions to caramelize for 35 minutes. Limit stirring but make sure the onions do not burn.

2. Slowly stir the stock into the onions. Add the wine, cognac, rosemary, thyme, and bay leaves. Increase the heat to medium-high and bring the stock to a boil. Cook it for 10 minutes, stirring often. Reduce the heat to low and simmer the stock for 5 minutes. Remove and discard the rosemary, thyme, and bay leaves.

3. Using a funnel and slotted spoon, evenly distribute the onions into each jar, about 2 cups per quart jar or 1 cup per pint jar. Ladle the broth into each jar, leaving a 1-inch headspace.

4. Wipe the jar rims with a washcloth dipped in vinegar. Place the lid and ring on each jar and hand tighten.

5. Process in a pressure canner at 10 PSI or according to your elevation and canner type. Process quart jars for 75 minutes and pint jars for 60 minutes.

INGREDIENTS

¼ cup butter

6 large sweet onions, sliced (9 cups)

1 large red onion, sliced (3 cups)

1 head garlic, peeled and crushed (¼ cup)

12 cups beef stock

2 cups cabernet sauvignon wine

¼ cup cognac

2 sprigs fresh rosemary

2 sprigs fresh thyme

3 bay leaves

Buffalo Chicken Dinner

A beloved American dish known for its bold and spicy flavor, this recipe can be made into your favorite appetizer or used in wraps and salads. It has the perfect amount of "kick" and is creamy and delicious even without dairy. Feel free to add cream cheese when reheating to serve.

PREP TIME: **10 minutes**   COOK TIME: **25 minutes**
PROCESS TIME: **90 or 75 minutes**   YIELD: **4 quarts or 8 pints**

DIRECTIONS

1. Fill a large pot halfway with water and add the chicken breasts. Bring it to a boil over medium-high heat and parboil the breasts for 5 minutes or until the exterior is cooked. Using tongs, remove the breasts and place them on a cutting board to cool. The chicken will not be cooked all the way through.

2. Place the oil in a stockpot and heat it on low heat. Add the bell pepper, onion, celery, and garlic, mix well to coat, and then sweat for 5 minutes to soften. Cube the chicken breasts into bite-size pieces, add them to the stockpot, and mix well. Stir in the coconut milk and bring it to a boil, then reduce the heat and simmer for 10 minutes, stirring often.

3. In a deep saucepan, melt the ghee over medium heat. Next, add the hot sauce, soy sauce, apple cider vinegar, and cayenne pepper. Whisk together and add to the stockpot with the chicken mixture. Mix well to evenly coat the chicken and vegetables and blend the ingredients.

4. Using a funnel, ladle the mixture into each jar, leaving 1 inch of headspace. Be sure to evenly distribute the sauce among the jars. Remove any trapped air pockets and add additional mixture if necessary to maintain the 1-inch headspace.

5. Wipe the jar rims with a washcloth dipped in vinegar. Place the lid and ring on each jar and hand tighten.

6. Process in a pressure canner at 10 PSI or according to your elevation and canner type. Process quart jars for 90 minutes and pint jars for 75 minutes.

INGREDIENTS

5½ lbs. boneless, skinless chicken breasts (15 cups)

1 T. olive oil

3 red bell peppers, diced (3 cups)

1 large onion, diced (1½ cups)

4 celery ribs, diced (1 cup)

6 garlic cloves, minced (1 T.)

2 cups coconut milk

½ cup ghee or butter

5 cups Frank's RedHot Original Hot Sauce

½ cup soy sauce or coconut aminos

3 T. apple cider vinegar

1 to 3 tsp. cayenne pepper (optional)

Campfire Breakfast Hash

This amazing breakfast is the perfect start to the day. Chorizo gives it a spicy flavor, which is offset by the sweetness of red bell peppers and starchy potatoes. We love using a quart jar for a Saturday morning breakfast accompanied by scrambled eggs with cheese and a steaming cup of coffee. However, it also makes for a great weeknight meal when I need something filling and quick.

PREP TIME: 15 minutes **COOK TIME:** 15 minutes
PROCESS TIME: 90 or 75 minutes **YIELD:** 5 quarts or 10 pints

DIRECTIONS

1. Place the chorizo in a stockpot and cook it over medium-high heat for 10 minutes, breaking the meat apart into smaller pieces with your spatula. Next, mix in the potatoes, peppers, corn, onion, and garlic. Cook the hash for an additional 5 minutes.

2. Dry pack the hash into each jar using a funnel and ladle filling each jar, leaving a 1-inch headspace.

3. Wipe the jar rims with a washcloth dipped in vinegar. Place the lid and ring on each jar and hand tighten.

4. Process in a pressure canner at 10 PSI or according to your elevation and canner type. Process quart jars for 90 minutes and pint jars for 75 minutes.

INGREDIENT TIP: *For a sweeter flavor to offset the spice, swap out the russet potatoes for an equal amount of sweet potatoes. If you wish to add more spicy heat to the recipe, add a teaspoon of cayenne pepper. You may also add 8 ounces of diced green chilies to the recipe to give it Tex-Mex flair.*

INGREDIENTS

3 lbs. ground chorizo

5 medium russet potatoes, peeled and cut into ½-inch cubes (5 cups)

5 red bell peppers, diced into ½-inch pieces (5 cups)

3 cups corn kernels, fresh or frozen

1 yellow onion, diced (1½ cups)

1 head garlic, peeled and minced (¼ cup)

Bratkartoffeln (German Fried Potatoes)

A staple in German cuisine, potatoes have been a part of German heritage since the seventeenth century. My cousin Lisa makes the best pan-fried version I've ever tasted. Pair these beauties with German schnitzel and a side of spaetzle for an amazing feast or eat them as a meal in itself. When you're ready to eat, simply panfry the potatoes in a bit of butter to crisp and lightly brown them.

PREP TIME: 25 minutes   **COOK TIME: 20 minutes**
PROCESS TIME: 40 or 35 minutes   **YIELD: 5 quarts or 10 pints**

INGREDIENTS

13 lbs. red skin potatoes, peeled

2 lbs. bacon, cut into 1-inch pieces (1½ cups)

2 yellow onions, diced (1½ cups)

1 cup chicken broth

¼ cup apple cider vinegar

2 tsp. salt (optional)

1 tsp. black pepper

1 tsp. paprika

DIRECTIONS

1. Partially fill a large bowl or pot with water. Chop the potatoes into 1-inch cubes, placing them in the bowl of water as you go. This will keep the potatoes from browning and will draw out excess starch. This should yield about 20 cups of chopped potatoes.

2. In a stockpot over medium-high heat, fry the bacon pieces for about 10 minutes or until the bacon is cooked but not burnt, stirring often. Use a slotted spoon to remove the bacon from the stockpot to cool. Keep the bacon grease in the stockpot and add the onion. Cook the onion for about 5 minutes or until it is translucent, then return the cooked bacon to the stockpot. Drain the potatoes and shake off excess water. Add the potatoes to the stockpot and mix well. Stir in the broth, vinegar, salt, pepper, and paprika. Cook for an additional 5 minutes.

3. Using a funnel, ladle the mixture into jars, leaving a 1-inch headspace. Be sure to tightly pack the mixture into each jar and evenly distribute any remaining liquid among the jars. The food will not be fully covered with liquid.

4. Wipe the jar rims with a washcloth dipped in vinegar. Place the lid and ring on each jar and hand tighten.

5. Process in a pressure canner at 10 PSI or according to your elevation and canner type. Process quart jars for 40 minutes and pint jars for 35 minutes.

Ground Turkey and Sweet Potato Mash

This sweet and spicy mash boasts an amazing combination of proteins and carbs. We often eat this recipe in the winter months when the snow is blistering and we need a bit of comfort. This also works well when I need an easy lunch, which is why I will often preserve this in pint jars that are perfect for individual servings.

PREP TIME: 15 minutes   **COOK TIME:** 20 minutes
PROCESS TIME: 90 or 75 minutes   **YIELD:** 5 quarts or 10 pints

DIRECTIONS

1. In a large stockpot, brown the turkey over medium-high heat for 10 minutes. Mix in the peppers, onion, jalapeño, and garlic. Cook the vegetables for an additional 5 minutes or until the onion starts to soften.

2. Place the broth and tomato paste in a small bowl and whisk them together, then add the mixture to the stockpot. Stir well to thoroughly coat the meat and vegetables. Cook for 5 minutes. Add the sweet potatoes, paprika, salt, pepper, and red pepper flakes and mix well.

3. Using a funnel, ladle the mash into jars, leaving a 1-inch headspace. Be sure to evenly distribute any remaining sauce among each jar. Remove any trapped air pockets. The food will not be fully covered with liquid.

4. Wipe the jar rims with a washcloth dipped in vinegar. Place the lid and ring on each jar and hand tighten.

5. Process in a pressure canner at 10 PSI or according to your elevation and canner type. Process quart jars for 90 minutes and pint jars for 75 minutes.

INGREDIENTS

4 lbs. ground turkey

2 red bell peppers, diced (2 cups)

1 red onion, diced (1½ cups)

1 jalapeño, seeds removed and finely chopped (½ cup)

1 head garlic, peeled and minced (¼ cup)

2 cups chicken broth

6 oz. tomato paste

1 lb. sweet potatoes, peeled and diced (4 cups)

1 T. paprika

2 tsp. salt (optional)

1 tsp. black pepper

1 to 3 tsp. red pepper flakes

Hungarian Mushroom Soup

Mushrooms have been an integral part of Hungarian cuisine for centuries due to the abundance of forest in the region. Mushrooms, both wild and cultivated, have long been valued for their earthy flavors and nutritional benefits. Enjoy this beloved, iconic dish encompassing flavors from sweet paprika and dill.

PREP TIME: 15 minutes   **COOK TIME:** 45 minutes
PROCESS TIME: 90 or 75 minutes   **YIELD:** 5 quarts or 10 pints

INGREDIENTS

¼ cup butter

3 T. olive oil

2 lbs. cremini mushrooms, sliced

2 lbs. white button mushrooms, sliced

2 yellow onions, diced (1½ cups)

1 cup white wine (chardonnay)

12 cups chicken broth

½ cup Worcestershire sauce

½ bunch fresh parsley, chopped (¾ cup)

3 T. fresh finely chopped dill

1 T. sweet Hungarian paprika

1 tsp. black pepper

DIRECTIONS

1. In a large stockpot, heat the butter and oil over medium heat until the butter fully melts. Add the mushrooms and cook them for 25 minutes or until they shrink in size by half. Stir in the onion and cook for an additional 5 minutes. Slowly add the wine, deglaze the pan, and cook for an additional 5 minutes or until the wine is reduced by half.

2. Stir in the broth, Worcestershire sauce, parsley, dill, paprika, and pepper. Increase the heat to medium high and bring the broth to a boil, then reduce the heat and simmer for 10 minutes, stirring often.

3. Using a funnel, ladle the soup into jars, leaving a 1-inch headspace.

4. Wipe the jar rims with a washcloth dipped in vinegar. Place the lid and ring on each jar and hand tighten.

5. Process in a pressure canner at 10 PSI or according to your elevation and canner type. Process quart jars for 90 minutes and pint jars for 75 minutes.

RECIPE TIP: *Give your soup its creamy texture prior to serving. Simply mix in a dollop of sour cream and a splash of whole milk when you're heating a jar or two on the stovetop.*

German Rouladen

This traditional German dish is made of thinly sliced beef rolled in a filling made from onions, mustard, pickles, and bacon. My mom and aunts often make this family tradition for the holidays. Though it is often braised in a skillet on the stovetop, we are going to sear the rolls, cover them with sauce, and preserve it in jars.

PREP TIME: 40 minutes   COOK TIME: 35 minutes
PROCESS TIME: 90 minutes   YIELD: 6 quarts or 12 pints

INGREDIENTS

6½ lbs. top round beef

1 cup yellow mustard

1½ lbs. bacon (24 slices)

12 German gherkin pickles, quartered lengthwise

2 large yellow onions, thinly sliced

Toothpicks or butcher's twine

5 T. olive oil, divided

¼ cup butter

6 carrots, peeled and finely chopped (3 cups)

2 parsnips, peeled and finely chopped (2 cups)

2 small leeks, finely chopped (2 cups)

1 head garlic, peeled and minced (¼ cup)

8 cups beef stock

2 cups red wine (merlot)

1 (6 oz.) can tomato paste

2 tsp. salt (optional)

1 tsp. black pepper

DIRECTIONS

1. Cut the beef into 24 slices measuring 4 × 6 inches with a ¼-inch thickness. Using a meat mallet and cutting board, gently pound out each beef slice until it decreases in thickness enough to increase the size to roughly 4½ by 7½ inches. Try not to pound it too thin creating holes.

2. Starting with 4 slices, lay each piece of pounded beef onto a cutting board. Spread each beef slice with a teaspoon or two of mustard. Next, place one strip of bacon lengthwise onto each beef slice. Add four pickle slices about an inch apart, then cover with a layer of onion slices.

3. Starting at the base of the longer side, begin to tuck and roll each beef slice upward being sure to tuck the outer sides of the width into the center to keep any filling from falling out. Fasten the rolls together with three toothpicks or tie each roll into place with butcher's twine. Repeat steps 2 and 3 until all 24 rolls have been made.

4. Heat the oil in a deep skillet or stockpot over medium-high heat. Working in batches, use tongs to add 4 rolls to the skillet and sear them for 1 minute on each side, then remove the rolls from the heat. In the same skillet, melt the butter. Add the carrots, parsnips, leeks, and garlic. Sauté for 5 minutes, using a spatula to scrape the beef bits off the bottom of the pan while stirring. Slowly add the stock, wine, tomato paste, salt (if using), and pepper and stir the sauce mixture until the paste dissipates. Bring the sauce to a boil for 5 minutes, stirring often. Remove from heat and set the pan aside.

5. Pack the beef rolls into each jar by tipping the jar on its side and laying the rolls on top of one another. Be gentle but be sure to fit 4 rolls into each quart jar and 2 rolls into each pint jar. Leave a minimum of 1 inch of headspace.

6. Stand the packed jars upright onto a cutting board. Using a funnel, ladle the sauce into each jar, being sure the sauce surrounds the rolls and leaves a 1-inch headspace. Remove any trapped air pockets and add additional sauce if necessary to maintain the 1-inch headspace.

7. Wipe the jar rims with a washcloth dipped in vinegar. Place the lid and ring on each jar and hand tighten.

8. Process in a pressure canner at 10 PSI or according to your elevation and canner type. Process quart jars for 90 minutes and pint jars for 75 minutes.

Savory Beef Cabbage Rolls

Cabbage rolls are a very common dish, spanning a variety of continents and many cultural adaptations dating back over 2,000 years. This Americanized version is made with seasoned beef and tomato sauce. Have fun adding your favorite herbs and spices to create the flavors you and your family love.

PREP TIME: 10 minutes **COOK TIME:** 30 minutes
PROCESS TIME: 90 or 75 minutes **YIELD:** 6 quarts or 12 pints

INGREDIENTS

1 head green cabbage

Filling

2 lbs. ground beef

1 sweet onion, diced (1½ cups)

1 head garlic, peeled and minced
(¼ cup)

1 T. dried marjoram

½ T. dried thyme

Sauce

2 cups tomato puree or sauce

2 cups beef broth

2 T. brown sugar

DIRECTIONS

1. Core the cabbage and remove its outer leaves. Place it in a deep pot and cover the cabbage with water. Bring it to a boil over medium-high heat, turning occasionally. After 5 to 10 minutes, as the outer leaves begin to fall from the head and become flexible, use tongs to gently pull the leaves off, one at a time, and set them aside on a plate to cool. For a single batch of this recipe, you will need about 24 cabbage leaves.

2. In a deep skillet, combine the ground beef, onion, garlic, marjoram, and thyme. Cook the beef mixture over medium-high heat for 10 minutes or until the meat is no longer pink. Set aside until it is cool to the touch.

3. In a saucepan, combine the tomato puree, broth, and sugar. Whisk the mixture together and bring it to a boil over medium-high heat. Reduce the heat to low and gently simmer the sauce for 5 minutes, stirring often and being sure not to scorch it. Set it aside.

4. To assemble the rolls, cut the thick part of the vein from the center of a cabbage leaf. Flatten the cabbage leaf and add ¼ cup of the beef filling at the base of the leaf in its center, spreading the filling up to a half inch from the end of the cabbage leaf. Tuck the sides of the leaf inward as you roll. Each roll will be a bit plump in shape, but do not overfill the rolls so you may fit as many as possible in each jar. Repeat this until all 24 leaves are filled and rolled.

5. Raw pack the stuffed cabbage rolls into each jar by tipping the jar on its side and laying the rolls on top of one another. Be gentle but fit as many rolls as you can; about 3 to 4 rolls in each quart jar and 2 to 3 rolls in each pint jar. Leave a minimum 1 inch of headspace in each jar.

6. Stand the packed jars upright onto a cutting board. Using a funnel, ladle the sauce into each jar, being sure the sauce surrounds the rolls and leaves 1 inch of headspace. Remove any trapped air pockets and add additional sauce if necessary to maintain the 1-inch headspace.

7. Wipe the jar rims with a washcloth dipped in vinegar. Place the lid and ring on each jar and hand tighten.

8. Process in a pressure canner at 10 PSI or according to your elevation and canner type. Process quart jars for 90 minutes and pint jars for 75 minutes.

INGREDIENT TIP: *Cabbage leaves rolled taller than the jar will not fit, so if you have a large head of cabbage, cut the leaf in half after removing the thick center vein to ensure the stuffed roll will fit into the jar and not exceed the 1-inch headspace.*

Seafood Pot Pie Filling

Also known as fish pie, this filling is reminiscent of a classic British comfort food that has a long-standing presence in British culinary traditions. Like other home-canned pie fillings, we create the base using a variety of ingredients so you may later heat a jar, add your cream or milk, and create a pie top with pie dough or puff pastry. Enjoy having this classic on your pantry shelf for a quick, versatile meal on the ready.

PREP TIME: **20 minutes** COOK TIME: **16 minutes**
PROCESS TIME: **160 or 110 minutes** YIELD: **5 quarts or 10 pints**

INGREDIENTS

¼ cup butter

1 yellow onion, diced (1½ cups)

4 celery ribs, diced (1 cup)

8 cups fish stock or vegetable broth, divided

1 cup white wine (pinot grigio or chardonnay)

4 medium white-flesh potatoes, peeled and cut into 1-inch cubes (4 cups)

4 carrots, peeled and diced (2 cups)

1 small fennel bulb, diced (2 cups)

1 cup green peas (fresh or frozen)

½ bunch fresh dill, finely chopped (½ cup)

2 tsp. dried tarragon

½ cup ClearJel

5 lbs. wild caught white fish, bones and skin removed and cut into 2-inch pieces (halibut, cod, haddock, sole)

DIRECTIONS

1. Melt the butter in a stockpot over medium-high heat. Add the onion and celery and cook for about 10 minutes or until the onion is translucent. Slowly stir in 7 cups of fish stock and the wine. Bring it to a boil. Add the potatoes, carrots, fennel, peas, dill, and tarragon and mix well. Return the mixture to a boil and allow it to boil for 5 minutes.

2. In a small bowl whisk together 1 cup of the fish stock and the ClearJel. Slowly add the mixture to the stockpot, stirring constantly, and allow it to boil for 1 minute, then remove from heat. (If the filling begins to get too thick while cooking, add water in ½ cup increments to achieve the desired consistency.)

3. Evenly distribute the raw fish among each jar. Using a funnel, ladle the filling into each jar leaving a generous 1-inch headspace. Remove any trapped air pockets and add additional filling if necessary to maintain the generous 1-inch headspace.

4. Wipe the jar rims with a washcloth dipped in vinegar. Place the lid and ring on each jar and hand tighten.

5. Process in a pressure canner at 10 PSI or according to your elevation and canner type. Process quart jars for 160 minutes and pint jars for 110 minutes.

White Bean and Sausage Stew

Thick and hearty, this amazing stew is the perfect meal to serve on a cold winter's night with a slice of warm bread fresh out of the oven. This is my mom's favorite as she will often enjoy it with oyster or soda crackers. Added to the many benefits of kale, the stew's simple ingredients are rich in protein.

PREP TIME: 80 minutes COOK TIME: 40 minutes
PROCESS TIME: 90 or 75 minutes YIELD: 7 quarts or 14 pints

DIRECTIONS

1. Thoroughly rinse the dried beans in a colander, being sure to remove any rocks, debris, or disfigured beans. Place the beans in a stockpot and cover them with water. Bring it to a boil over high heat, and allow the beans to boil for 10 minutes. Remove from heat, cover the stockpot, and steep the beans for 1 hour.

2. Place the oil, carrot, onion, celery, and garlic in a stockpot and cook over medium-high heat for 10 minutes or until the onion starts to brown. Add the sausage and cook it until the meat is no longer pink, about 10 minutes.

3. Empty the beans into a colander in the sink and quickly rinse them. Add to the stockpot the beans, chicken stock, water, thyme, salt, and pepper and mix well. Bring it to a boil, then reduce the heat and simmer the stew for 5 minutes. Using tongs, remove the thyme sprigs from the stockpot. Strip the leaves off the thyme sprigs and place them into the stockpot, discarding the stems. Add the kale, mix well, and simmer the stew for an additional 5 minutes, then remove from heat.

4. Using a funnel and slotted spoon, fill each jar ¾ full of the bean and meat mixture. Next, ladle the stock into each jar, leaving 1 inch of headspace. Remove any trapped air pockets and add additional stock if necessary to maintain the 1-inch headspace.

5. Wipe the jar rims with a washcloth dipped in vinegar. Place the lid and ring on each jar and hand tighten.

6. Process in a pressure canner at 10 PSI or according to your elevation and canner type. Process quart jars for 90 minutes and pint jars for 75 minutes.

INGREDIENTS

- 2 cups dried navy or great northern beans or 4 (15 oz.) cans beans
- 2 T. olive oil
- 4 carrots, peeled and diced (2 cups)
- 1 large onion, diced (1½ cups)
- 4 celery ribs, diced (1½ cups)
- 1 head garlic, peeled and minced (¼ cup)
- 2 lbs. ground sausage, spicy or savory
- 8 cups chicken stock
- 4 cups water
- 4 sprigs fresh thyme
- 2 tsp. salt (optional)
- 1 tsp. black pepper
- ½ bunch kale, chopped (6 cups)

Fish (Not Tuna)

Both fresh and saltwater fish can be safely preserved using a pressure canner. Perfect candidates for canning include catfish, northern pike, salmon, smelt, and trout. If the fish is frozen, thaw it completely in the refrigerator before canning.

PREP TIME: **30 minutes**   COOK TIME: **0 minutes**
PROCESS TIME: **160 or 100 minutes / 7 quarts, or 14 pints, or 28 half-pints**

INGREDIENTS

14 lbs. fish (do not use Tuna)
14 tsp. salt (optional)

INGREDIENT TIP: *For larger fish, remove the bones and fat from skinned fillets and cut fillets into 2- or 3-inch pieces. Smaller fish, like smelt, are canned whole with their heads and tails removed. Roughly one pound of fish will fill one wide-mouth pint jar.*

DIRECTIONS

1. Bones and skin can be removed or left in, except for halibut, which must have the bones and skin removed prior to canning. (The skin of halibut is too tough to consume, but its bones are excellent for making fish stock.)

2. Cut filleted fish into 2- or 3-inch pieces and dry pack the fish tightly into jars, leaving a 1-inch headspace. If desired, you may add 2 teaspoons of salt to each quart jar, 1 teaspoon to each pint, and ½ teaspoon to each half-pint jar. Do **not** add water.

3. Wipe the jar rims with a washcloth dipped in vinegar. Place the lid and ring on each jar and hand tighten.

4. Fill the pressure canner with 3 quarts of cool water, or according to the manufacturer's specifications. Add the jars to the pressure canner and heat canner slowly using medium-high heat for 15 minutes. Then increase the heat to high and operate as usual.

5. Process in a pressure canner at 10 PSI or according to your elevation and canner type. Process quart jars for 160 minutes and pint and half-pint jars for 100 minutes.

SERVING TIP: *After canning and during storage, it is common to see glass-like crystals form on the fish, especially salmon. This is normal and what you are seeing is magnesium ammonium phosphate. The crystals will dissolve when heated and are safe to eat.*

Meatloaf

While meatloaf is a traditional German, Scandinavian, and Belgian dish, it made its way into the homes of Americans back in colonial times, starting in Pennsylvania in 1870. Often a mixture of ground pork or beef with cornmeal or breadcrumbs, it was popular during wartime as a means to sustain and stretch a tight budget. Enjoy having ready-to-eat meatloaf in a jar with this delicious canning recipe. This recipe works best with a wide-mouth jar for easy removal.

PREP TIME: 20 minutes   COOK TIME: none
PROCESS TIME: 90 or 75 minutes   YIELD: 5 wide-mouth quarts or 10 wide-mouth pints

DIRECTIONS

1. Place the ground beef in a large bowl and break it apart in sections using a rubber spatula. Add the onion and garlic and mix well to combine. Beat the egg yolks in a small bowl, then add them to the beef mixture, mixing well to combine. Mix in the breadcrumbs and Worcestershire sauce.

2. In a small bowl, combine the paprika, mustard, oregano, basil, salt (if using), thyme, and pepper. Sprinkle the seasonings over the beef mixture, then mix well to evenly combine the ingredients.

3. Raw pack the jars, leaving 1 inch of headspace. Be sure to tightly pack each jar, ensuring there are no air pockets.

4. Wipe the jar rims with a washcloth dipped in vinegar. Place the lid and ring on each jar and hand tighten.

5. Process in a pressure canner at 10 PSI or according to your elevation and canner type. Process quart jars for 90 minutes and pint jars for 75 minutes.

SERVING TIP: *When you're ready to heat and serve this meal in a jar, use a butter knife to encircle the meatloaf, releasing it from the interior of the jar. Cut it into slices and heat it in a skillet. When serving, feel free to create a yummy sauce by whisking together ketchup, mustard, and brown sugar and heating the sauce through on the stovetop.*

INGREDIENTS

12 lbs. ground beef or pork

2 yellow onions, finely chopped (2½ cups)

1 head garlic, peeled and minced (¼ cup)

3 egg yolks

1½ cups breadcrumbs

¼ cup Worcestershire sauce

2 T. paprika

1 T. ground mustard

1 T. dried oregano

1 T. dried basil

2 tsp. salt (optional)

1 tsp. dried thyme

1 tsp. black pepper

9

Middle Eastern Cuisine

The enchanting world of Middle Eastern cuisine is a tapestry woven with flavors, traditions, and centuries of culinary excellence. Spanning diverse cultures and geographical landscapes, which transcend the borders of Lebanon, Egypt, Turkey, Iran, and Cyprus, Middle Eastern cuisine encompasses an extraordinary fusion of aromatic spices, vibrant colors, and tantalizing textures. From the bustling streets of Istanbul to the majestic deserts of Saudi Arabia and the fertile valleys of Lebanon, the region's cuisine is a captivating expression of history, culture, and shared experiences.

Middle Eastern cuisine has a rich heritage deeply rooted in ancient civilizations that have left an indelible mark on the culinary landscape. Millennia-old trade routes connected the East and the West, facilitating the exchange of goods, ideas, and culinary practices.

Common ingredients used in abundance in this cuisine are olives, honey, sesame seeds, mint, chickpeas, and parsley. Other fresh herbs such as turmeric and saffron lend their vibrant flavors and colors to recipes, while spices like cumin, coriander, and cardamom infuse dishes with warmth and depth.

Olive oil, dates, and nuts are cherished staples, adding richness and complexity to countless recipes, while vegetables such as squash, eggplant, okra, and carrots provide texture and nutrition. Protein comes in different forms throughout the region. In addition to the traditional lamb and chicken, alternative sources of protein come from garbanzo beans, lentils, and black-eyed peas.

Learn how to preserve a variety of meals in a jar such as bamya okra stew, Jewish minestrone, Persian turmeric chicken, and Turkish stuffed cabbage rolls, just to name a few.

Baharat Lebanese Chicken

This recipe may appear simplistic, but it is loaded with flavor. Using seven of the predominant ground spices known in Middle Eastern cuisine, this recipe is the perfect main course to highlight any meal. Serve it alongside a colorful salad and with a side of couscous with golden raisins for a complete meal in minutes.

PREP TIME: **10 minutes**   COOK TIME: **20 minutes**
PROCESS TIME: **90 or 75 minutes**   YIELD: **5 quarts or 10 pints**

INGREDIENTS

35 to 40 boneless, skin-on 4 oz. chicken thighs, excess skin removed

Salt and pepper

4 T. olive oil, divided

1 cup slivered almonds

1 cup pine nuts

1 T. ground coriander

1 T. ground cumin

½ T. ground nutmeg

½ T. paprika

2 tsp. ground cinnamon

1 tsp. cardamom

1 tsp. salt (optional)

½ tsp. ground cloves

½ tsp. black pepper

2 lemons, thinly sliced and seeds removed

1 large red onion, thinly sliced (3 cups)

DIRECTIONS

1. Pat the chicken dry with a paper towel and sprinkle each thigh with a dash of salt and pepper on both sides. Heat 1 tablespoon of the oil in a deep skillet over medium-high heat. Working in batches, add the chicken to the skillet with the skin-side down and fry for 5 minutes or until it turns golden brown, being careful not to overcrowd the skillet. Remove from heat.

2. Using the same skillet, add any remaining oil, almonds, and pine nuts. Toss and lightly toast the nuts over medium-high heat for about 5 minutes. Remove them from the skillet and place the nuts in a small bowl. Set it aside.

3. In a separate small bowl, whisk together the coriander, cumin, nutmeg, paprika, cinnamon, cardamom, salt, cloves, and black pepper.

4. Place the thighs in a large baking dish and sprinkle the thighs with half of the seasoning mix, flip them over, and sprinkle the other side with the remaining seasoning mix. Next, disperse the toasted nuts over the thighs.

5. Raw pack about 7 to 8 coated thighs per quart jar or 3 to 4 coated thighs per pint jar, leaving a generous 1-inch headspace. Add the lemon and onion slices after each thigh, layering as you go. Be sure all the toasted nuts are evenly distributed among the jars as well.

6. Wipe the jar rims with a washcloth dipped in vinegar. Place the lid and ring on each jar and hand tighten.

7. Process in a pressure canner at 10 PSI or according to your elevation and canner type. Process quart jars for 90 minutes and pint jars for 75 minutes.

Chicken Shawarma in a Jar

Likely one of the most-known Middle Eastern recipes among food enthusiasts, this meal in a jar is packed full of flavor using an array of spices. While most shawarma is either baked or grilled, we will be cooking it in its natural juices and spices during processing. When you're ready to open a jar to eat, spread the chicken onto a cookie sheet and roast it in the oven at 425°F (218°C) for 10 to 15 minutes to heat through and crisp. Serve it with a side of tabouleh and hummus with pita bread loaded with fresh veggies.

PREP TIME: 10 minutes   **COOK TIME: 12 minutes**
PROCESS TIME: 90 or 75 minutes   **YIELD: 6 quarts or 12 pints**

DIRECTIONS

1. Heat 2 tablespoons of the oil in a skillet over medium-high heat. Working in batches, brown the chicken for 2 minutes on each side, being careful not to overcrowd the skillet. Place chicken in a large bowl to cool.

2. In a small bowl, whisk together the seasonings. Cover the chicken with the remaining 2 tablespoons of the oil and mix well to coat. Sprinkle the seasonings atop the chicken and mix well to thoroughly coat the meat. Let it sit for 5 minutes, then mix well again.

3. Using a funnel, ladle the chicken into each jar, leaving a generous 1-inch headspace.

4. Wipe the jar rims with a washcloth dipped in vinegar. Place the lid and ring on each jar and hand tighten.

5. Process in a pressure canner at 10 PSI or according to your elevation and canner type. Process quart jars for 90 minutes and pint jars for 75 minutes.

INGREDIENTS

4 T. olive oil, divided

5 lbs. boneless, skinless chicken breasts, cut into 2-inch pieces (15 cups)

4 ½ lbs. boneless, skinless chicken thighs, cut into 2-inch pieces (9 cups)

2 T. ground cumin

2 T. ground turmeric

2 T. ground coriander

2 T. garlic powder

2 tsp. paprika

1 tsp. ground cloves

1 to 3 tsp. cayenne pepper

1 tsp. salt (optional)

Bamya (Okra) Stew

Bamya is the Arabic word for okra, and this stew is loaded with this nutritious vegetable. This meal is found in households all over the Middle East and is often served over rice. It is a deliciously simple meal with an earthy flavor, perfect for those who prefer a lighter meal without protein.

PREP TIME: **10 minutes**   **COOK TIME:** **20 minutes**
PROCESS TIME: **40 or 35 minutes**   **YIELD:** **8 quarts or 16 pints**

DIRECTIONS

1. Place the oil, onion, and garlic in a stockpot and mix well. Cook over medium heat, or until the onion is translucent, about 10 minutes. Stir in the okra, tomatoes, and salt (if using), and cook the vegetables for an additional 5 minutes. Increase the heat to medium high and add the stock, bay leaves, coriander, and turmeric. Mix well. Bring it to a boil and allow the soup to boil for 5 minutes. Remove and discard the bay leaves.

2. Using a funnel, ladle the soup into jars, leaving a 1-inch headspace.

3. Wipe the jar rims with a washcloth dipped in vinegar. Place the lid and ring on each jar and hand tighten.

4. Process in a pressure canner at 10 PSI or according to your elevation and canner type. Process quart jars for 40 minutes and pint jars for 35 minutes.

INGREDIENTS

2 T. olive oil

2 yellow onions, diced (3 cups)

1 head garlic, peeled and minced (¼ cup)

3 lbs. fresh okra, sliced into rounds (13½ cups)

9 Roma tomatoes, diced (3 cups)

1 tsp. salt (optional)

16 cups vegetable stock

4 bay leaves

1 T. ground coriander

1 T. ground turmeric

Chunky Lentil Soup

My mom is famous in our home for making the best lentil soups. She loves to get creative by adding carrots and tomatoes. Taking it one step further, I added additional vegetables and Middle Eastern spices to create a fun recipe you may serve as a first course to any dinner or you may enjoy a bowl as a meal all on its own.

PREP TIME: 30 minutes **COOK TIME:** 20 minutes
PROCESS TIME: 90 or 75 minutes **YIELD:** 9 quarts or 18 pints

INGREDIENTS

3 T. olive oil

1 yellow onion, diced (1½ cups)

1 head garlic, peeled and minced (¼ cup)

12 cups chicken or vegetable broth

12 cups water

5 parsnips, peeled and diced (4 cups)

3 medium sweet potatoes, peeled and diced (3 cups)

½ head green cabbage, shredded (3 cups)

2 zucchini, diced (2½ cups)

4 carrots, peeled and chopped (2 cups)

4 celery ribs, diced (1 cup)

½ bunch fresh parsley, finely chopped (½ cup)

1 T. seven spice

2 tsp. paprika

2 cups dried red, green, or brown lentils

DIRECTIONS

1. In a stockpot over medium-high heat, place the oil, onion, and garlic and cook until the onion is soft, about 5 minutes. Stir in the remaining ingredients, except the lentils, and bring the soup to a boil, then reduce the heat and simmer for 15 minutes, stirring often. Add the lentils, mix well, and simmer for an additional 5 minutes.

2. Using a funnel and slotted spoon, fill each jar to ¾ full with the vegetable mixture. Do not tap down ingredients. Next, ladle the broth into each jar, leaving a 1-inch headspace.

3. Wipe the jar rims with a washcloth dipped in vinegar. Place the lid and ring on each jar and hand tighten.

4. Process in a pressure canner at 10 PSI or according to your elevation and canner type. Process quart jars for 90 minutes and pint jars for 75 minutes.

Chickpea Stew

Enjoy this rich, warm stew flavored with za'atar (pronounced zaah-tar). This amazing Middle Eastern spice blend is a beautiful combination of herbs including mint, sesame seeds, sumac, and salt. It has a nutty, zesty tang to it and is delicious on just about everything!

PREP TIME: 80 minutes COOK TIME: 25 minutes
PROCESS TIME: 90 or 75 minutes YIELD: 8 quarts or 16 pints

INGREDIENTS

1 lb. dried chickpeas

2 T. olive oil

1 large eggplant, cubed (4½ cups)

4 red bell peppers, diced (4 cups)

1 yellow onion, diced (1½ cups)

2-inch gingerroot, peeled and minced (2 T.)

12 garlic cloves, minced (2 T.)

6 Roma tomatoes, diced (2 cups)

16 cups vegetable broth

2 T. za'atar

1 T. ground cumin

1 T. paprika

2 tsp. red pepper flakes (to taste)

2 tsp. salt (optional)

DIRECTIONS

1. Thoroughly rinse the dried chickpeas in a colander, being sure to remove any rocks, debris, or disfigured beans. Place the chickpeas in a stockpot and cover them with water. Bring it to a boil over high heat, and allow the chickpeas to boil for 10 minutes. Remove from heat, cover the stockpot, and steep the chickpeas for 1 hour.

2. In a stockpot over medium-high heat, mix the oil, eggplant, bell peppers, onion, ginger, and garlic. Cook for 10 minutes, stirring often, or until the onion is translucent.

3. Empty the steeped chickpeas into a colander in the sink and rinse. Add the chickpeas, tomatoes, broth, and spices to the stockpot and mix well. Bring the stew to a boil and cook for 5 minutes, stirring occasionally.

4. Using a funnel, ladle the stew into jars, leaving a 1-inch headspace. Remove any trapped air pockets and add additional stew if necessary to maintain the 1-inch headspace.

5. Wipe the jar rims with a washcloth dipped in vinegar. Place the lid and ring on each jar and hand tighten.

6. Process in a pressure canner at 10 PSI or according to your elevation and canner type. Process quart jars for 90 minutes and pint jars for 75 minutes.

Cypriot Pork Tavas

Representing a traditional culinary style from Cyprus, tavas *is all about slow cooking. Often performed in clay pots, these one-pot meals consist of meat, vegetables, and herbs slowly cooked to meld together and intensify the flavors. What better way for us canners to accomplish this than in a glass mason jar? Serve it atop couscous or steamed jasmine rice.*

PREP TIME: 25 minutes   COOK TIME: none
PROCESS TIME: 90 or 75 minutes   YIELD: 7 quarts or 14 pints

DIRECTIONS

1. In a large bowl or stockpot, combine the pork, potato, carrot, tomato, and onion. Pour the oil over the mixture and mix well to coat. Sprinkle the mixture with the oregano, cumin, and black pepper and mix well to blend the seasonings. Let the ingredients sit for 5 minutes, then mix well again.

2. Fill each jar using a funnel and a large spoon, leaving a 1-inch headspace.

3. Wipe the jar rims with a washcloth dipped in vinegar. Place the lid and ring on each jar and hand tighten.

4. Process in a pressure canner at 10 PSI or according to your elevation and canner type. Process quart jars for 90 minutes and pint jars for 75 minutes

RECIPE TIP: *This recipe is dry packed using raw ingredients and will make its own juices during processing. When filling the jars, be sure to pack the ingredients tightly into each jar to maximize the jar space.*

INGREDIENTS

3 lbs. pork shoulder, cut into 2-inch pieces (10 cups)

6 medium potatoes, peeled and chopped into 2-inch cubes (6 cups)

9 carrots, peeled and chopped into 1-inch-thick rounds (5 cups)

9 Roma tomatoes, quartered (4 cups)

1 large red onion, roughly chopped (3 cups)

¼ cup olive oil

2 T. dried oregano

1 T. ground cumin

1 tsp. black pepper

Deconstructed Stuffed Onions

The traditional version of this recipe is to stuff a large onion and pan roast it until it is golden brown. When working with a pressure canner and the confines of a glass mason jar, we must get creative to enjoy this delicious take on a traditional recipe. Bask in the sweetness of pearl onions cooked in a delicious mixture of meat, pine nuts, and spices from the Middle East.

PREP TIME: 30 minutes   **COOK TIME: 20 minutes**
PROCESS TIME: 90 or 75 minutes   **YIELD: 6 quarts or 12 pints**

DIRECTIONS

1. Place the lamb, garlic, and za'atar in a stockpot and cook them over medium-high heat for 10 minutes or until the meat is browned and fully cooked. Add the pine nuts and cook for an additional 5 minutes, mixing well. Stir in the tomatoes, broth, and paste. Cook the mixture for an additional 5 minutes.

2. Measure out 2½ cups of onions for each quart jar or 1¼ cups for each pint jar, then set the onions aside. Using a funnel and large spoon, add a first layer of ½ cup of the meat mixture to each jar, followed by 2 to 3 pearl onions, and repeat the layers until the jars are full, leaving 1 inch of headspace. Be sure to pack down the meat mixture each time prior to adding the onions.

3. Wipe the jar rims with a washcloth dipped in vinegar. Place the lid and ring on each jar and hand tighten.

4. Process in a pressure canner at 10 PSI or according to your elevation and canner type. Process quart jars for 90 minutes and pint jars for 75 minutes.

INGREDIENTS

5 lbs. ground lamb or beef

1 head garlic, peeled and minced (¼ cup)

2 T. za'atar

1 cup pine nuts

6 Roma tomatoes, diced (2 cups)

1 cup chicken or vegetable broth

1 (6 oz.) can tomato paste

20 oz. pearl onions, peeled (13 cups)

Ghormeh Sabzi (Persian Herb Stew)

The origins of **ghormeh sabzi** *can be traced back to the era of the Persian Empire, where it was enjoyed by the nobility and royalty. Over time, the dish's popularity spread throughout the region, becoming a beloved staple in Persian households and an essential part of Iranian cuisine.*

PREP TIME: 80 minutes COOK TIME: 35 minutes
PROCESS TIME: 90 or 75 minutes YIELD: 7 quarts or 14 pints

INGREDIENTS

- 2 cups dried kidney beans or 3 (15 oz.) cans kidney beans
- ¼ cup olive oil
- 2 large yellow onions, diced (4 cups)
- 1 head garlic, peeled and minced (¼ cup)
- 2 T. ground turmeric
- 3 lbs. lamb shoulder or beef chuck roast, cut into 2-inch pieces (10 cups)
- 2 bunches fresh spinach leaves (24 oz.), stems removed and coarsely chopped (4 cups)
- 2 bunches fresh parsley, finely chopped (2 cups)
- 1 bunch fresh cilantro, finely chopped (1 cup)
- 1 bunch fresh fenugreek leaves, finely chopped (1 cup)
- 14 dried Persian limes
- 8 cups beef broth
- 4 cups water

INGREDIENT TIP: *If you do not have access to Persian dried limes, you may use your personally dehydrated limes (wedged or whole) for this recipe. After heating a jar or two on the stovetop, discard the dried limes before serving.*

DIRECTIONS

1. Thoroughly rinse the dried beans in a colander, being sure to remove any rocks, debris, or disfigured beans. Place the beans in a stockpot and cover them with water. Bring to a boil over high heat, and allow the beans to boil for 10 minutes. Remove from heat, cover the stockpot, and steep the beans for 1 hour.

2. Place the oil, onion, and garlic in a separate stockpot and cook them over medium-high heat for 10 minutes or until the onion starts to brown. Add the turmeric and mix well. Add the lamb pieces, mix well to coat, and cook the meat for about 10 minutes or until it is lightly browned.

3. Empty the steeped beans (or canned beans) into a colander in the sink and quickly rinse them. Add the beans, spinach, parsley, cilantro, fenugreek, limes, broth, and water to the stockpot and mix well. Bring it to a boil, then reduce the heat and simmer the stew for 5 minutes.

4. Using a funnel and slotted spoon, retrieve 2 dried limes from the stockpot and add them to each quart jar and 1 to each pint jar, then fill jars with the meat mixture, pressing down to pack the jars well as you fill them, leaving a 1-inch headspace. Ladle broth into each jar keeping the 1-inch headspace. Remove any trapped air pockets and add additional broth if necessary to maintain the 1-inch headspace.

5. Wipe the jar rims with a washcloth dipped in vinegar. Place the lid and ring on each jar and hand tighten.

6. Process in a pressure canner at 10 PSI or according to your elevation and canner type. Process quart jars for 90 minutes and pint jars for 75 minutes.

Iranian Carrots and Black-Eyed Peas

Delight in a hearty mixture of protein and vegetables with this amazingly flavored and colorful recipe. This combination provides a well-rounded meal, hitting all the senses. Serve it over saffron basmati rice with a dash of salt and pepper or enjoy it in a bowl all on its own.

PREP TIME: **25 minutes**   COOK TIME: **none**
PROCESS TIME: **90 or 75 minutes**   YIELD: **7 quarts or 14 pints**

DIRECTIONS

1. Thoroughly rinse the dried peas in a colander, being sure to remove any rocks, debris, or disfigured peas. Place the peas in a stockpot and cover them with water. Using your hands, agitate the peas in the water to remove any dirt. Empty the peas into the colander and rinse them again. If you're using canned peas, empty them into a colander and rinse.

2. In a large stockpot, combine the peas, carrots, bell peppers, tomatoes, parsley, and ginger and mix thoroughly. Sprinkle the cumin and turmeric over the mixture and continue to mix well.

3. Using a funnel, ladle the mixture into each jar, leaving a generous 1 inch of headspace. Pack the ingredients down to ensure you maximize jar space and maintain the generous 1-inch headspace. Next, ladle the water or broth into the jars, leaving 1 inch of headspace. Remove any trapped air pockets by gently tapping the jar bottom on a cutting board. Add additional water or broth to maintain the 1-inch headspace.

4. Wipe the jar rims with a washcloth dipped in vinegar. Place the lid and ring on each jar and hand tighten.

5. Process in a pressure canner at 10 PSI or according to your elevation and canner type. Process quart jars for 90 minutes and pint jars for 75 minutes.

INGREDIENTS

1 cup dried black-eyed peas, or 2 (15 oz.) cans black-eyed peas

8 lbs. carrots, peeled and chopped (20 cups)

4 red bell peppers, diced (4 cups)

6 Roma tomatoes, diced (2 cups)

1 bunch fresh parsley, finely chopped (1 cup)

1-inch gingerroot, peeled and minced (1 T.)

1 T. ground cumin

1 T. ground turmeric

25 cups water or vegetable broth

Israeli Eggplant with Lamb

Eggplant in Israeli cuisine is deeply rooted in the cultural and culinary traditions of the region. Eggplant, or aubergine, has been cultivated in the Middle East for thousands of years. The versatility of eggplant and its ability to absorb flavors and textures makes it a very popular ingredient in Middle Eastern dishes.

PREP TIME: 15 minutes   **COOK TIME:** 30 minutes
PROCESS TIME: 90 or 75 minutes   **YIELD:** 6 quarts or 12 pints

INGREDIENTS

2 T. olive oil

1 cup pine nuts

1 large sweet onion, diced (2 cups)

6 lbs. ground lamb, venison, or beef

2 large eggplants, cubed (9 cups)

6 Roma tomatoes, diced (2 cups)

1 cup golden raisins or chopped dates

2 cups beef broth

1 (6 oz.) can tomato paste

2 T. ground cinnamon

1 T. ground cumin

2 tsp. sumac

1 tsp. ground nutmeg

DIRECTIONS

1. Heat the oil in a stockpot over medium-high heat. Add the pine nuts and brown them for 2 minutes. Add the onion and cook the mixture for about 8 minutes or until the onion is translucent. Add the ground lamb and break it into small pieces with a spatula. Cook the lamb for about 10 minutes or until it is browned and cooked through.

2. Add the eggplant, tomatoes, raisins, broth, tomato paste, cinnamon, cumin, sumac, and nutmeg to the stockpot and mix well. Cook the mixture for an additional 10 minutes, stirring often.

3. Using a funnel, ladle the mixture into jars, leaving a 1-inch headspace. Remove any trapped air pockets and add additional filling if necessary to maintain the 1-inch headspace.

4. Wipe the jar rims with a washcloth dipped in vinegar. Place the lid and ring on each jar and hand tighten.

5. Process in a pressure canner at 10 PSI or according to your elevation and canner type. Process quart jars for 90 minutes and pint jars for 75 minutes.

RECIPE TIP: *Make Stuffed Eggplant. Preheat the oven to 425°F (218°C), cut an eggplant in half lengthwise, scoop out the center pulpy flesh, and brush the cut side with olive oil. Bake it cut side up for 20 minutes or until browned. Heat a quart jar of the Israeli eggplant with lamb in a saucepan, then fill the eggplant with the mix, cover it with foil, and return it to the oven for an additional 30 minutes.*

Jewish Minestrone

The perfect soup to warm you from the inside out on cold, damp days with little sun. This filling soup is loaded with aromatics, vegetables, and plenty of beans. It receives its depth from chicken stock and fresh herbs. When you're ready to serve it, pop open a jar, heat it in a saucepan, and add your favorite pasta topped with freshly grated Parmesan cheese.

PREP TIME: 85 minutes **COOK TIME:** 35 minutes
PROCESS TIME: 85 or 55 minutes **YIELD:** 7 quarts or 14 pints

INGREDIENTS

1 cup dried kidney beans, or
   2 (15 oz.) cans kidney beans

2 T. olive oil

6 carrots, diced (3 cups)

1 yellow onion, diced (1½ cups)

4 celery ribs, diced (1 cup diced)

1 head garlic, peeled and minced
   (¼ cup)

½ bunch fresh parsley, chopped
   (½ cup)

½ head green cabbage, shredded
   (3 cups)

2 zucchini, diced (2½ cups)

6 Roma tomatoes, diced (2 cups)

2 medium sweet potatoes, peeled
   and cubed (2 cups)

14 cups chicken stock

3 sprigs fresh oregano

3 sprigs fresh thyme

DIRECTIONS

1. Thoroughly rinse the dried beans in a colander, being sure to remove any rocks, debris, or disfigured beans. Place the dried beans in a stockpot and cover them with water. Bring to a boil over high heat and allow the beans to boil for 10 minutes. Remove from heat, cover the stockpot, and steep the beans for 1 hour.

2. Place the oil, carrot, onion, celery, garlic, and parsley in a stockpot and cook the vegetables over medium-high heat for 10 minutes or until the onion is translucent. Add the cabbage, mix well, and cook the vegetables for 5 minutes or until the cabbage softens.

3. Empty the steeped beans (or canned beans) into a colander in the sink and quickly rinse them. Add the beans, zucchini, tomatoes, sweet potatoes, chicken stock, oregano, and thyme sprigs to the stockpot and mix well. Bring it to a boil, and allow the mixture to boil for 5 minutes. Reduce the heat and simmer the mixture for an additional 5 minutes.

4. Using a funnel and slotted spoon, fill each jar ¾ full with the vegetable-bean mixture. Do not tightly pack the mixture down. Next, ladle the soup stock into each jar, leaving 1 inch of headspace.

5. Wipe the jar rims with a washcloth dipped in vinegar. Place the lid and ring on each jar and hand tighten.

6. Process in a pressure canner at 10 PSI or according to your elevation and canner type. Process quart jars for 85 minutes and pint jars for 55 minutes.

Lebanese Kofta Meatballs

*Kofta (or kufta/koofteh) originates from Persian culinary traditions which means "to grind." Often made into elongated shapes like a log or small loaf, you may also create this popular dish into round meatballs. While **kofta** is very versatile and is enjoyed by many cultures, this variation boasts a Middle Eastern flair due to cumin, cinnamon, allspice, coriander, and parsley. Enjoy it served with saffron rice and a green salad, or stuff it into a pita with hummus, fresh tomato slices, and cucumbers.*

PREP TIME: 10 minutes   **COOK TIME: 25 minutes**
PROCESS TIME: 90 or 75 minutes   **YIELD: 5 quarts or 10 pints**

DIRECTIONS

1. Preheat the oven to 450°F (232°C) and place the rack in the top third of the oven. Line a rimmed baking sheet with aluminum foil or use an oven-safe baking rack inside the baking sheet.

2. Mix all ingredients together in a large bowl. Form the meat mixture into 1½-inch balls, yielding about 90 meatballs. Line the meatballs onto the baking sheet in a single layer and place it in the oven.

3. Bake the meatballs for 20 minutes or until they are firm, flipping them once halfway through. Turn on the broiler and broil the meatballs for 5 minutes or until they are browned. Remove from heat and set them aside until they are cool to the touch.

4. Evenly distribute the meatballs within each jar, about 8 to 10 per quart jar and 5 to 6 per pint jar, leaving 1 inch of headspace.

5. Wipe the jar rims with a washcloth dipped in vinegar. Place the lid and ring on each jar and hand tighten.

6. Process in a pressure canner at 10 PSI or according to your elevation and canner type. Process quart jars for 90 minutes and pint jars for 75 minutes.

INGREDIENT TIP: *If you prefer a little "kick" to your meatballs, feel free to add 1 to 3 teaspoons of red pepper flakes or cayenne pepper to your meat mixture prior to forming it into meatballs.*

INGREDIENTS

3 lbs. lean ground beef

2 lbs. ground lamb

2 egg yolks

1 cup breadcrumbs

8 sprigs fresh parsley, finely chopped (¼ cup)

1 T. ground cumin

½ T. ground cinnamon

2 tsp. ground allspice

2 tsp. ground coriander

½ tsp. salt (optional)

Persian Turmeric Chicken

Soon to be a favorite in your home, this simple recipe is bursting with earthy citrus flavors. Coupled with delicious vegetables and dried Persian lime powder, this meal in a jar will help get dinner on the table in minutes. Simply heat a jar or two in a saucepan and serve it atop a bed of basmati rice with fresh lime wedges.

PREP TIME: 20 minutes **COOK TIME:** 15 minutes
PROCESS TIME: 90 or 75 minutes **YIELD:** 7 quarts or 14 pints

INGREDIENTS

3 T. olive oil

1 large onion, sliced (2 cups)

½ bunch fresh cilantro, chopped (½ cup)

6 garlic cloves, minced (1 T.)

7 lbs. boneless, skinless chicken thighs, cut into 1-inch pieces (14 cups)

1 medium turnip (1 lb.), peeled and diced (4 cups)

10 radishes, diced (1 cup)

2 T. ground turmeric

1 T. Persian dried lime powder

2 tsp. ground cumin

2 tsp. ground cardamom

1 tsp. salt (optional)

8 cups chicken broth

DIRECTIONS

1. Combine the oil, onion, cilantro, and garlic in a stockpot and cook them over medium-high heat for 5 minutes or until the onion is translucent. Stir in the chicken, turnip, radish, turmeric, lime powder, cumin, cardamom, and salt (if using) and cook for an additional 10 minutes, stirring often.

2. Using a funnel, ladle the chicken mixture into each jar, leaving 1 inch of headspace. Be sure to pack the chicken mixture tightly into each jar. Next, ladle the broth into each jar, leaving 1 inch of headspace. Remove any trapped air pockets and add additional broth if necessary to maintain the 1-inch headspace.

3. Wipe the jar rims with a washcloth dipped in vinegar. Place the lid and ring on each jar and hand tighten.

4. Process in a pressure canner at 10 PSI or according to your elevation and canner type. Process quart jars for 90 minutes and pint jars for 75 minutes.

Spicy Lamb Stew

This gorgeous stew is filled with protein for a hearty meal in a bowl in minutes. The caramelized onion creates its delicious base while the cayenne pepper gives it a spicy kick. Not feeling like lamb? No worries. This same stew can be made with a beef roast or a loin of pork— just be sure to use beef stock to keep the stew's amazing flavor and rich color.

PREP TIME: 30 minutes   COOK TIME: 45 minutes
PROCESS TIME: 90 or 75 minutes   YIELD: 7 quarts or 14 pints

DIRECTIONS

1. Heat 2 tablespoons of the oil in a stockpot over high heat. Working in batches, add the lamb to the stockpot and sear each side for 20 seconds, being careful not to overcrowd the stockpot. Remove lamb from heat and set aside.

2. In the same stockpot, add the remaining 2 tablespoons of oil and allow it to heat for 1 minute. Add the onion and mix well to coat in the oil. Reduce the heat to medium low and cook the onion for 10 minutes, stirring occasionally. Sprinkle the sugar, salt, and a dash of water onto the onion, mix well, and continue to cook for an additional 20 minutes or until the onion is caramelized, stirring occasionally. Add the garlic, mix well, and cook for an additional 5 minutes.

3. Slowly stir 1 cup of beef stock into the caramelized onion, scraping any bits off the bottom of the stockpot. Add the potatoes, tomatoes, bell peppers, tomato paste, cumin, coriander, cayenne pepper, cinnamon, and clove. Mix well and cook it for 5 minutes, then slowly pour in the remainder of the stock and add the seared lamb. Bring it to a boil, then reduce the heat and simmer the stew for 5 minutes.

4. Using a funnel, ladle the stew into each jar, leaving 1 inch of headspace. Remove any trapped air pockets and add additional stew if necessary to maintain the 1-inch headspace.

5. Wipe the jar rims with a washcloth dipped in vinegar. Place the lid and ring on each jar and hand tighten.

6. Process in a pressure canner at 10 PSI or according to your elevation and canner type. Process quart jars for 90 minutes and pint jars for 75 minutes.

INGREDIENTS

4 T. olive oil, divided

3 lbs. boneless lamb shoulder, cut into 2-inch chunks (10 cups)

1 red onion, diced (2 cups)

2 tsp. sugar

1 tsp. salt

1 dash of water

1 head garlic, peeled and minced (¼ cup)

8 cups beef stock, divided

6 yellow potatoes, cubed (6 cups)

6 Roma tomatoes, diced (2 cups)

2 medium red bell peppers, diced (2 cups)

1 (6 oz.) can tomato paste

2 T. ground cumin

1 T. ground coriander

1 to 3 tsp. cayenne pepper

1 tsp. ground cinnamon

½ tsp. ground cloves

Turkish Stuffed Cabbage Rolls

Known as **mahshi malfouf** *in the Middle East, these stuffed cabbage rolls are filled with a delicious mixture of meat, pine nuts, and cauliflower rice and smothered in an herb-infused tomato sauce. I made a few fun tweaks to ensure we have the right outcome in a jar and am happy to say that I have found my new favorite meal in a jar recipe.*

PREP TIME: **10 minutes**   COOK TIME: **30 minutes**
PROCESS TIME: **90 or 75 minutes**   YIELD: **6 quarts or 12 pints**

INGREDIENTS

1 head green cabbage

Filling

2 lbs. ground beef or lamb

1 cup cauliflower rice, fresh or frozen

½ cup pine nuts

1 head garlic, peeled and minced (¼ cup)

Sauce

1 (32 oz.) can tomato juice

1 (6 oz.) can tomato paste

½ bunch fresh parsley, finely chopped (¼ cup)

1 T. seven spice blend

1 T. granulated sugar

DIRECTIONS

1. Core the cabbage and remove its outer leaves. Place it in a deep pot and cover it with water. Bring it to a boil over medium-high heat, turning occasionally. After 5 to 10 minutes, as the outer leaves begin to fall from the head and become flexible, use tongs to gently pull a leaf off, one at a time, and set them aside on a plate to cool. For a single batch of this recipe, you will need about 36 cabbage leaves.

2. In a deep skillet, combine the ground beef, cauliflower rice, pine nuts, and garlic. Cook the mixture over medium-high heat for about 10 minutes or until the meat is no longer pink. Set it aside.

3. In a saucepan, whisk together the tomato juice, tomato paste, parsley, seven spice, and sugar. Bring it to a boil over medium-high heat. Reduce the heat to low and gently simmer the sauce for 5 minutes, stirring often and being sure not to scorch it. Set the sauce aside.

4. To assemble, cut the thick part of the vein from the center of the cabbage leaf. Flatten the cabbage leaf and add 2 tablespoons of filling at the base of the leaf in its center, spreading the filling to about a half inch from the end of the cabbage leaf. Tuck the sides of the leaf inward as you roll. Each roll should look like the shape of a cigar. Repeat this until all 36 leaves are filled and rolled.

5. Raw pack the stuffed cabbage rolls into jars by tipping each jar on its side and laying the rolls on top of one another. Be gentle but be sure to fit as many rolls as you can; about 5 to 6 rolls in each quart jar and 3 to 4 rolls in each pint jar. Leave a minimum of 1 inch of headspace in each jar.

6. Stand the packed jars upright on a cutting board. Using a funnel, ladle the tomato sauce into each jar, being sure the sauce surrounds the rolls and leaves a 1-inch headspace. Remove any trapped air pockets and add additional sauce if necessary to maintain the 1-inch headspace.

7. Wipe the jar rims with a washcloth dipped in vinegar. Place the lid and ring on each jar and hand tighten.

8. Process in a pressure canner at 10 PSI or according to your elevation and canner type. Process quart jars for 90 minutes and pint jars for 75 minutes.

Vegetarian Cuisine

Diets relying on vegetables, beans, and legumes are growing in popularity and becoming a way of life for many people. For canners who wish to create delicious, hearty meals without meat or meat byproducts, this chapter is for you.

We will explore creative recipes using wholesome grains, legumes, and vibrant vegetables as well as luscious fruits, nuts, and aromatic herbs, showcasing the incredible versatility and culinary potential of plant-based ingredients. This chapter has been thoughtfully curated to showcase the bounty of flavors, textures, and colors nature provides. I have carefully crafted a variety of dishes to cater to a range of tastes and dietary preferences. Each recipe has been designed to not only nourish your body but also excite your palate, proving vegetarian cuisine is both delicious and satisfying.

By incorporating a variety of plant-based proteins, such as legumes, tofu, tempeh, and plant-based meat substitutes, you can reach your daily protein needs without relying on animal sources. Additionally, the fiber content in plant-based foods supports healthy digestion and can help prevent constipation. It also provides a feeling of satiety, which can aid in maintaining a healthy weight. The diverse array of nutrients found in vegetarian diets nourishes your body and promotes overall vitality.

Explore the endless possibilities of vegetarian canning, unlocking the potential of ingredients that will inspire creativity and bring joy to your home canning adventures. Get ready to celebrate the richness of plant-based ingredients and savor every bite as we dive into the exciting world of vegetarian cuisine with recipes such as jackfruit sloppy joes, vegetable marsala, and bean and barley soup.

Bean and Barley Soup

This hearty soup is loaded with protein and vegetables with a hint of barley, providing nourishment and texture. Rich in flavor, feel free to use dried herbs of your liking to achieve the result you desire. You may also substitute water for vegetable broth or simply use tomato juice as the soup's base.

PREP TIME: 80 minutes   COOK TIME: 45 minutes

PROCESS TIME: 90 or 75 minutes   YIELD: 7 quarts or 14 pints

DIRECTIONS

1. Thoroughly rinse the dried beans in a colander, being sure to remove any rocks, debris, or disfigured beans. Place the dried beans in a stockpot and cover them with water. Bring to a boil over high heat, and allow the beans to boil for 10 minutes. Remove from heat, cover the stockpot, and steep the beans for 1 hour.

2. In a stockpot, heat the oil on medium-high heat. Add the onion and cook until translucent, about 10 minutes, stir often to avoid burning. Add the carrots, celery, and garlic to the stockpot, mix well, and cook for an additional 5 minutes.

3. Empty the steeped beans (or canned beans) into a colander in the sink and quickly rinse them. Add the broth to the stockpot with the vegetables and mix well, then add the beans, tomatoes, bay leaves, salt (if using), and pepper. Bring it to a boil, then reduce the heat and simmer the soup for 20 minutes, stirring often.

4. Add 1 tablespoon of barley to each quart jar and a ½ tablespoon to each pint jar. Using a funnel, ladle the soup into each jar, leaving a 1-inch headspace.

5. Wipe the jar rims with a washcloth dipped in vinegar. Place the lid and ring on each jar and hand tighten.

6. Process in a pressure canner at 10 PSI or according to your elevation and canner type. Process quart jars for 90 minutes and pint jars for 75 minutes.

INGREDIENT TIP: *While hulled barley has a higher nutritional value and can withstand longer exposure to high temperature, you may substitute pearled barley for this recipe with great results.*

INGREDIENTS

- 1 lb. dried cannellini beans (2 cups) or 4 (15 oz.) cans cannellini beans
- 2 T. olive oil
- 2 sweet onions, diced (4 cups)
- 6 carrots, peeled and diced (3 cups)
- 6 celery ribs, diced (1½ cups)
- 1 head garlic, peeled and minced (¼ cup)
- 14 cups vegetable broth
- 6 Roma tomatoes, diced (2 cups)
- 2 bay leaves
- 2 tsp. salt (optional)
- 1 tsp. black pepper
- ½ cup hulled barley

Bhindi Masala

Bhindi masala is an Indian dish made of stir-fried okra, tomatoes, and spices. Okra, also known as lady's-finger, is a very popular vegetable in India. This delicious recipe boasts amazing flavor using ginger, coriander, and turmeric. Serve it hot with a side of rice or lentils.

PREP TIME: 25 minutes   COOK TIME: 25 minutes
PROCESS TIME: 40 or 35 minutes   YIELD: 5 quarts or 10 pints

INGREDIENTS

4 T. olive oil, divided

1 large red onion, finely chopped (2½ cups)

1 head garlic, peeled and minced (¼ cup)

4-inch gingerroot, peeled and finely chopped (¼ cup)

1 T. cumin seeds

3 lbs. fresh okra, patted dry and cut into 1-inch rounds (12 cups)

9 Roma tomatoes, diced (3 cups)

2 T. ground coriander

1 to 3 T. Kashmiri red chili powder

1 T. ground turmeric

1 T. dried mango powder (optional)

1 tsp. salt (optional)

4 cups vegetable broth

DIRECTIONS

1. In a stockpot, heat 2 tablespoons of the oil over medium-high heat. Add the onion, garlic, ginger, and cumin seeds and cook them for about 10 minutes or until the onion is translucent. Add the remaining 2 tablespoons of oil and the okra, toss, and heat the mixture through for 10 minutes or until the okra softens.

2. Add the tomatoes, coriander, chili powder, turmeric, mango powder, and salt (if using) to the stockpot and mix well. Slowly add the vegetable broth, increase the heat, and bring it to a boil. Allow the mixture to boil for 5 minutes. Stir well, then remove from heat.

3. Using a funnel, ladle the okra mixture into each jar, leaving a 1-inch headspace. Remove any trapped air pockets and add additional mixture if necessary to maintain the 1-inch headspace.

4. Wipe the jar rims with a washcloth dipped in vinegar. Place the lid and ring on each jar and hand tighten.

5. Process in a pressure canner at 10 PSI or according to your elevation and canner type. Process quart jars for 40 minutes and pint jars for 35 minutes.

INGREDIENT TIP: *If you wish to use the dried mango powder but do not have access to it, feel free to add 2 tablespoons of lime juice to the recipe.*

Black Bean Chili

This meatless chili still packs a wallop when it comes to a hearty helping of protein and fiber. Boasting all the traditional flavors of chili, it is sure to please. Made with a mixture of black beans, red kidney beans, and chipotle peppers in adobo sauce, it has the right amount of heat and flavor. Top it with sour cream and sliced jalapeño when you're ready to serve.

PREP TIME: 75 minutes   **COOK TIME:** 40 minutes
PROCESS TIME: 90 or 75 minutes   **YIELD:** 6 quarts or 12 pints

DIRECTIONS

1. Thoroughly rinse the dried beans in a colander, being sure to remove any rocks, debris, or disfigured beans. Place the beans in a stockpot and cover them with water. Bring it to a boil over high heat and allow the beans to boil for 10 minutes. Remove from heat, cover the stockpot, and steep the beans for 1 hour.

2. Heat the oil in a separate stockpot and over medium-high heat. Add the onion, carrot, bell pepper, jalapeño, and garlic and cook them for 10 minutes or until the onion is translucent. Empty the steeped beans (or canned beans) into a colander in the sink and rinse them. Add the beans, tomatoes, chipotles, cilantro, chili powder, cumin, and salt (if using). Bring it to a boil, then reduce the heat and simmer the chili for 20 minutes, stirring often.

3. Using a funnel, ladle the chili into jars, leaving a 1-inch headspace. Remove any trapped air pockets and add additional chili if necessary to maintain the 1-inch headspace.

4. Wipe the jar rims with a washcloth dipped in vinegar. Place the lid and ring on each jar and hand tighten.

5. Process in a pressure canner at 10 PSI or according to your elevation and canner type. Process quart jars for 90 minutes and pint jars for 75 minutes.

INGREDIENTS

- 1 cup dried black beans or 4 (15 oz.) cans black beans
- 1 cup dried red kidney beans or 3 (15 oz.) cans kidney beans
- 2 T. olive oil
- 1 sweet onion, diced (1½ cups)
- 4 carrots, peeled and diced (2 cups)
- 2 red bell peppers, diced (2 cups)
- 1 jalapeño, minced (½ cup)
- 1 head garlic, peeled and minced (¼ cup)
- 36 Roma tomatoes, diced (12 cups)
- 4 oz. canned chipotles with sauce, minced
- ½ bunch fresh cilantro, finely chopped (½ cup)
- ½ cup chili powder
- ⅛ cup ground cumin
- 2 tsp. salt (optional)

INGREDIENT TIP: *Looking to add additional protein and texture to your chili? Feel free to decrease to 1 cup of dried beans in the recipe and replace it with 2 pounds of soy-based vegan meat. Cook it through in step 2, before adding the onion and remaining ingredients.*

Indian Lentil Curry

Preserving curried dal in a jar is a fun way to quicken the cooking time in the kitchen. Heating a jar through on the stovetop will take much less time as the lentils will break down easier after being pressure canned. Serve this flavorful meal over a bed of rice or couscous or with a side of naan bread.

PREP TIME: 10 minutes   COOK TIME: 20 minutes
PROCESS TIME: 90 or 75 minutes   YIELD: 5 quarts or 10 pints

INGREDIENTS

12 cups vegetable broth

12 cups water

2 yellow onions, finely chopped (2½ cups)

6 Roma tomatoes, diced (2 cups)

1 head garlic, peeled and minced (¼ cup)

3-inch gingerroot, peeled and minced (3 T.)

4 green chilies, deseeded and chopped

1 T. crushed dried mint leaves

2 tsp. turmeric powder

1 tsp. garam masala

1 tsp. ground cumin

1 tsp. salt (optional)

1 lb. dried yellow lentils (2½ cups)

DIRECTIONS

1. Combine the broth, water, onion, tomato, garlic, ginger, chilies, mint, turmeric, garam masala, cumin, and salt (if using) in a large stockpot and bring it to a boil over medium-high heat. Reduce the heat and simmer the broth mixture for 15 minutes.

2. Thoroughly rinse the lentils in a colander, being sure to remove any rocks, debris, or disfigured lentils. Add the lentils to the stockpot. Mix well and simmer for an additional 5 minutes.

3. Using a funnel and slotted spoon, fill each quart jar with 4 inches of the lentil mixture and each pint jar with 2 inches of the lentil mixture. Be sure to tightly pack each jar before measuring the height of the lentils with a ruler on the outside of the jar.

4. Ladle the broth into each jar, leaving a 1-inch headspace. Remove any trapped air pockets and add additional liquid if necessary to maintain the 1-inch headspace.

5. Wipe the jar rims with a washcloth dipped in vinegar. Place the lid and ring on each jar and hand tighten.

6. Process in a pressure canner at 10 PSI or according to your elevation and canner type. Process quart jars for 90 minutes and pint jars for 75 minutes.

INGREDIENT TIP: *If you would like your curry to be a bit hotter, leave the seeds in the chilies. Also, if you have access to curry leaves, feel free to include 16 leaves when creating the soup base in step 1. The curry leaves may be kept in the jars or removed prior to filling the jars, per your preference.*

Black-Eyed Pea Stew

A healthy solution when a quick and filling meal is needed, this stew has it all. This colorful stew is loaded with bell peppers, sweet potatoes, and kale, which complement the beauty of the black-eyed peas. Seasoned with fresh herbs, this meal in a jar is for any occasion.

PREP TIME: 80 minutes   **COOK TIME:** 25 minutes
PROCESS TIME: 90 or 75 minutes   **YIELD:** 7 quarts or 14 pints

INGREDIENTS

1 lb. dried black-eyed peas
(2 cups)

2 T. olive oil

1 yellow onion, diced (1½ cups)

1 red bell pepper, diced (1 cup)

1 green bell pepper, diced (1 cup)

12 garlic cloves, minced (2 T.)

16 cups vegetable broth

1 bunch fresh kale, destemmed
and chopped (6 cups)

4 medium sweet potatoes, peeled
and cut into ½-inch cubes
(4 cups)

4 sprigs fresh thyme

1 to 2 tsp. red pepper flakes
(to taste)

2 tsp. salt (optional)

DIRECTIONS

1. Thoroughly rinse the dried peas in a colander, being sure to remove any rocks, debris, or disfigured peas. Place the peas in a stockpot and cover them with water. Bring it to a boil over high heat and allow the beans to boil for 10 minutes. Remove from heat, cover the stockpot, and steep the peas for 1 hour.

2. Combine the oil, onion, bell pepper, and garlic in a separate stockpot and cook the vegetables over medium-high heat for 10 minutes or until the onion is translucent, stirring often. Empty the steeped peas into a colander in the sink and rinse them. Add the peas, broth, kale, sweet potatoes, thyme, red pepper flakes, and salt to the stockpot. Mix well. Bring it to a boil, and allow the stew to boil for 5 minutes, stirring occasionally.

3. Using a funnel and slotted spoon, fill each jar to ¾ full with the pea mixture. Next, ladle the stew liquid into each jar, leaving 1 inch of headspace. Remove any trapped air pockets and add additional stew liquid if necessary to maintain the 1-inch headspace.

4. Wipe the jar rims with a washcloth dipped in vinegar. Place the lid and ring on each jar and hand tighten.

5. Process in a pressure canner at 10 PSI or according to your elevation and canner type. Process quart jars for 90 minutes and pint jars for 75 minutes.

Cacciatore

Cacciatore is an Italian style of cooking associated with a rustic hunter's stew and is typically served with meat; however, this vegetarian version is sure to please. The jackfruit soaks in the robust and earthy flavors of its rich tomato-based sauce while the vegetables and mushrooms give this stew a pleasing texture. Enjoy served over garlic mashed potatoes, polenta, or steamed rice.

PREP TIME: **25 minutes**   **COOK TIME:** **30 minutes**
PROCESS TIME: **65 or 55 minutes**   **YIELD:** **7 quarts or 14 pints**

DIRECTIONS

1. Heat the oil in a stockpot over medium-high heat. Add the bell pepper, mushrooms, onion, celery, and garlic and mix well. Cook the vegetables for 10 minutes or until the onion is translucent and the peppers begin to soften.

2. Add the jackfruit, tomato juice, tomatoes, wine, oregano, basil, thyme, rosemary, salt (if using), and pepper and mix well. Bring it to a boil, then reduce the heat and simmer the mixture for 15 minutes, stirring often. Add the tomato paste and sugar and stir until the paste has fully dispersed and the stew has thickened. Simmer the stew for an additional 5 minutes, then remove it from heat.

3. Using a funnel, ladle the stew into jars, leaving a 1-inch headspace. Remove any trapped air pockets and add additional stew if necessary to maintain the 1-inch headspace.

4. Wipe the jar rims with a washcloth dipped in vinegar. Place the lid and ring on each jar and hand tighten.

5. Process in a pressure canner at 10 PSI or according to your elevation and canner type. Process quart jars for 65 minutes and pint jars for 55 minutes.

INGREDIENTS

3 T. oil

3 green bell peppers, chopped (3 cups)

9 oz. white mushrooms, sliced (3 cups)

2 yellow onions, chopped (2 cups)

4 celery ribs, diced (1 cup)

1 head garlic, peeled and minced (¼ cup)

5 (14 oz.) cans young jackfruit, drained and rinsed (9 cups)

64 oz. tomato juice (8 cups)

6 Roma tomatoes, diced (2 cups)

1 cup red wine (cabernet or malbec)

1 T. dried oregano

1 T. dried basil

1 tsp. dried thyme

1 tsp. dried crushed rosemary

1 tsp. salt (optional)

1 tsp. black pepper

1 (6 oz.) can tomato paste

1 T. brown sugar

Jackfruit Sloppy Joes

This fun all-American classic has gone meatless! Thanks to jackfruit, vegetarians may enjoy preserving this classic in their pantry for years to come. With all the same fun flavors of traditional sloppy joes, this recipe is delicious and hearty. Serve on your favorite style of bun and top with coleslaw or avocado slices.

PREP TIME: 10 minutes   **COOK TIME:** 15 minutes
PROCESS TIME: 75 or 55 minutes   **YIELD:** 5 quarts or 10 pints

DIRECTIONS

1. In a large stockpot, combine the jackfruit, onion, bell pepper, and garlic. Cook them over medium-high heat for 5 minutes, working to break apart the jackfruit as it cooks. Add the tomato sauce, broth, brown sugar, vinegar, Worcestershire Sauce, and mustard and mix well. Cook the mixture for an additional 10 minutes, stirring often.

2. Using a funnel, ladle the mixture into jars, leaving a 1-inch headspace. Remove any trapped air pockets and add additional mixture if necessary to maintain the 1-inch headspace.

3. Wipe the jar rims with a washcloth dipped in vinegar. Place the lid and ring on each jar and hand tighten.

4. Process in a pressure canner at 10 PSI or according to your elevation and canner type. Process quart jars for 75 minutes and pint jars for 55 minutes.

INGREDIENT TIP: *If you can only find jackfruit in brine, be sure to thoroughly rinse the jackfruit and soak it for 30 to 60 minutes in cold water, then rinse it a second time before using it in the recipe. If you fail to rinse brined jackfruit, it will have an unpleasant, overly salty taste that will likely ruin the recipe.*

INGREDIENTS

- 7 (14 oz.) cans young jackfruit in water, drained
- 2 sweet onions, finely chopped (2 cups)
- 1 green bell pepper, finely chopped (1 cup)
- 6 garlic cloves, minced (1 T.)
- 4 cups tomato sauce
- 2 cups vegetable broth
- ¼ cup packed brown sugar
- ¼ cup apple cider vinegar
- 3 T. Worcestershire sauce
- 1 T. yellow mustard

Portobella and Chickpea Supper

This delicious meal in a jar is the perfect solution when you are craving mushrooms. Filled to the brim with flavorful portobella mushrooms and spinach leaves, this dish is accompanied by chickpeas and a pinch of red pepper flakes. Simply heat it and serve a quart for supper alongside a slice of crusty bread.

PREP TIME: 70 minutes **COOK TIME: 35 minutes**
PROCESS TIME: 90 or 75 minutes **YIELD: 6 quarts or 12 pints**

INGREDIENTS

1½ cups dried chickpeas or 3 (15 oz.) cans chickpeas

3 T. olive oil

2 yellow onions, diced (2 cups)

1 head garlic, peeled and minced (¼ cup)

1 T. dried basil leaves

1 T. dried oregano

1 tsp. dried thyme

1 T. coconut aminos

1 to 3 tsp. red pepper flakes (to taste)

32 oz. portobella mushrooms, sliced (8 cups)

3 red bell peppers, diced (3 cups)

10 oz. fresh spinach leaves (10 cups)

10 cups vegetable broth or water

DIRECTIONS

1. Thoroughly rinse the dried chickpeas in a colander, being sure to remove any rocks, debris, or disfigured chickpeas. Place the dried chickpeas in a stockpot and cover them with water. Bring it to a boil over high heat, and allow the chickpeas to boil for 10 minutes. Remove from heat, cover the stockpot, and steep for 1 hour.

2. In a stockpot over medium-high heat, combine the oil, onion, garlic, basil, oregano, thyme, coconut aminos, and red pepper flakes. Cook for 10 minutes or until the onion is translucent, stirring often. Empty the steeped chickpeas (or canned chickpeas) into a colander in the sink and rinse them. Add the chickpeas, mushrooms, and peppers. Mix well. Bring it to a boil and cook for 5 minutes, stirring occasionally. Add the spinach and broth. Return it to a boil, and allow everything to boil gently for 10 minutes or until the spinach has started to wilt and has reduced in size by half.

3. Using a funnel and slotted spoon, fill each jar until it is ¾ full of the mixture. Next, ladle the liquid into each jar, leaving 1 inch of headspace. Remove any trapped air pockets and add additional liquid if necessary to maintain the 1-inch headspace.

4. Wipe the jar rims with a washcloth dipped in vinegar. Place the lid and ring on each jar and hand tighten.

5. Process in a pressure canner at 10 PSI or according to your elevation and canner type. Process quart jars for 90 minutes and pint jars for 75 minutes.

Pumpkin Chili

Chili is a cool-weather favorite for so many. This vegetarian chili is the perfect fall-weather treat, proudly displaying the many ingredients, colors, and flavors of fall. The warm undertones of cinnamon blend beautifully with the sweetness of pumpkin and the earthiness of beans. After preserving this treasure, you'll certainly be coming back for more.

PREP TIME: 35 minutes   COOK TIME: 25 minutes
PROCESS TIME: 90 or 75 minutes   YIELD: 7 quarts or 14 pints

INGREDIENTS

3 T. olive oil

1 yellow onion, diced (1½ cups)

2 bell peppers, diced (2 cups)

1 to 2 jalapeños, finely chopped (1 cup)

1 head garlic, peeled and minced (¼ cup)

64 oz. tomato puree (8 cups)

2 cups vegetable broth

6 Roma tomatoes, diced (2 cups)

2 small pie pumpkins, peeled, seeded, and cut into 1-inch pieces (9 cups)

3 (15 oz.) cans kidney beans, drained and rinsed

¼ cup chili powder

1 T. ground cumin

1 T. brown sugar

2 tsp. ground cinnamon

1 tsp. salt (optional)

DIRECTIONS

1. Combine the oil, onion, bell pepper, jalapeño, and garlic in a stockpot and mix well. Over medium-high heat, cook the vegetables for 10 minutes or until the onion becomes translucent, stirring occasionally. Add the tomato puree, broth, tomatoes, pumpkin, beans, chili powder, cumin, sugar, cinnamon, and salt (if using) and mix well. Bring it to a boil, then reduce the heat and simmer the chili for 15 minutes.

2. Using a funnel, ladle the chili into jars, leaving a 1-inch headspace. Remove any trapped air pockets and add additional chili if necessary to maintain the 1-inch headspace.

3. Wipe the jar rims with a washcloth dipped in vinegar. Place the lid and ring on each jar and hand tighten.

4. Process in a pressure canner at 10 PSI or according to your elevation and canner type. Process quart jars for 90 minutes and pint jars for 75 minutes.

INGREDIENT TIP: *This recipe calls for canned beans, either store bought or home canned. If you wish to use dried beans, they will need to be soaked in water for a minimum of 4 hours, up to 8 hours maximum, then rinsed before being used in this recipe. Given the amount of acid in this recipe, without presoaking the dried beans, they may not soften during processing.*

Roasted Carrot Soup

The vibrant hue of carrots harmonizes delightfully with the freshness of thyme and garlic. However, the true magic unfolds during the tender roasting of carrots, coaxing out their natural sugars and infusing each spoonful with luscious caramel depth. Serve hot with a dollop of sour cream and garnish with chopped chives or shaved Parmesan cheese.

PREP TIME: 15 minutes   **COOK TIME:** 75 minutes   **PROCESS TIME:** 75 or 60 minutes   **YIELD:** 7 quarts or 14 pints

DIRECTIONS

1. Preheat the oven to 425°F (218°C).
2. Arrange the carrots in a single layer on two baking sheets, then drizzle them with oil. Roast the carrots for 30 to 45 minutes or until they caramelize on the tops and edges. Using a spatula, carefully scrape the carrots and drippings into a large stockpot.
3. Add the onions, celery, broth, water, garlic, thyme, salt (if using), and pepper to the stockpot and bring to a boil over medium-high heat. Stir often to avoid scorching. Boil for 5 minutes, then reduce the heat to low, cover, and simmer for 30 minutes. Remove from heat.
4. Using a handheld stick immersion blender, or by working in batches using a food processor, puree the soup until everything is well blended.
5. Using a funnel, ladle the soup into jars, leaving a 1-inch headspace.
6. Wipe the jar rims with washcloth dipped in vinegar. Place the lid and ring on each jar and hand tighten.
7. Process in a pressure canner at 10 PSI or according to your elevation and canner type. Process quart jars for 75 minutes and pint jars for 60 minutes.

INGREDIENT TIP: *Want to add a bit of gingery zing to your soup? Peel and finely chop a 3-inch piece of gingerroot and add it to the stockpot with the other ingredients in step 3. The burst of ginger adds warmth and beautifully complements the natural sweetness of the carrots.*

INGREDIENTS

- 10 lbs. carrots, peeled, halved and rough chopped
- 4 T. olive oil
- 2 large onions, peeled and quartered
- 5 celery ribs
- 8 cups vegetable broth
- 4 cups water
- 8 whole garlic cloves
- 2 T. fresh thyme leaves
- 2 tsp. salt (optional)
- 1 tsp. black pepper

Ratatouille

This French classic dish is a chunky stew derived from a combination of six popular vegetables and fresh herbs. Typically baked in the oven, this version is preserved in a jar so you may partake whenever your heart desires. Serve it alongside a slice of freshly baked bread.

PREP TIME: 30 minutes   **COOK TIME: 15 minutes**
PROCESS TIME: 75 or 55 minutes   **YIELD: 5 quarts or 10 pints**

DIRECTIONS

1. Place the oil in a stockpot and heat it over medium-high heat. Add the onion and cook for 5 minutes, undisturbed, so it browns slightly. Stir in the eggplant, tomato, zucchini, bell pepper, basil, garlic, thyme, and red pepper flakes. Reduce the heat to medium and allow the mixture to cook for 10 minutes or until the tomatoes and peppers have released their juices, stirring occasionally.

2. Using a funnel, ladle the mixture into jars, leaving a generous 1¼-inch headspace. Remove any trapped air pockets and add additional mixture if necessary to maintain the 1¼-inch headspace.

3. Wipe the jar rims with a washcloth dipped in vinegar. Place the lid and ring on each jar and hand tighten.

4. Process in a pressure canner at 10 PSI or according to your elevation and canner type. Process quart jars for 75 minutes and pint jars for 55 minutes.

RECIPE TIP: *Create baked ratatouille using two quart jars and a 9 x 9-inch baking dish. Preheat oven to 425°F (220°C). Empty both jars into the baking dish and spread with a spoon to evenly coat. Next, sprinkle with 2 teaspoons of Herbes de Provence. Bake for 25 minutes or until the sauce is bubbling. Remove from oven and sprinkle 1½ cups shredded Gruyere cheese over the top and return it to the oven to bake for an additional 10 minutes, or until the cheese is melted and slightly golden brown.*

INGREDIENTS

3 T. olive oil

1 yellow onion, diced (1½ cups)

2 large eggplants, cut into 1-inch cubes (9 cups)

20 Roma tomatoes, diced (5 cups)

4 zucchini, cut into 1-inch cubes (5 cups)

3 orange bell peppers, diced (3 cups)

14 fresh basil leaves, coarsely chopped (⅓ cup)

1 head garlic, peeled and chopped (¼ cup)

6 fresh thyme sprigs, leaves stripped from stem

1 to 3 tsp. red pepper flakes (optional)

Spicy Chickpeas and Potatoes

While many spice this dish with cumin, we are using yellow curry and cayenne pepper to give it a punch of flavor and a bit of heat. If you're not a fan of curry, you may omit it from the recipe and replace it with a seasoning of your choice. This simplistic yet filling recipe makes for a great main course, or it may be served as a side dish.

INGREDIENTS

4½ cups dried chickpeas or 6 (15 oz.) cans chickpeas

3 T. olive oil

1 large red onion, diced (3 cups)

6 celery ribs, diced (1½ cups)

1 green bell pepper, finely chopped (¾ cup)

1 head garlic, peeled and minced (¼ cup)

8 cups vegetable broth or water

6 gold or white potatoes, cut into 1-inch cubes (6 cups)

2 T. yellow curry powder

2 to 4 tsp. cayenne pepper

1 tsp. red pepper flakes

1 tsp. salt (optional)

½ tsp. black pepper

RECIPE TIP: *The broth in each jar will be soaked up by your chickpeas, making this thicker, like a casserole. If you wish to thin it out prior to serving it, add additional water or vegetable broth to the saucepan when heating the meal on the stovetop.*

PREP TIME: 90 minutes   COOK TIME: 25 minutes
PROCESS TIME: 90 or 75 minutes   YIELD: 4 quarts or 8 pints

DIRECTIONS

1. Thoroughly rinse the dried chickpeas in a colander, being sure to remove any rocks, debris, or disfigured chickpeas. Place the chickpeas in a stockpot and cover them with water. Bring to a boil over high heat, and allow the chickpeas to boil for 10 minutes. Remove from heat, cover the stockpot, and steep the chickpeas for 1 hour.

2. In a stockpot over medium-high heat, combine the oil, onion, celery, bell pepper, and garlic. Cook the vegetables over medium-high heat for 10 minutes or until the onion is translucent, stirring often. Empty the steeped chickpeas (or canned chickpeas) into a colander in the sink and rinse them. Add the chickpeas, broth, potatoes, curry, cayenne, red pepper flakes, salt, and pepper. Mix well and bring the broth to a boil. Cook 5 more minutes, stirring occasionally.

3. Using a funnel and slotted spoon, fill each jar with the chickpea mixture, leaving 2 inches of headspace. Next, ladle the broth into each jar, leaving 1 inch of headspace. Remove any trapped air pockets and add additional broth if necessary to maintain the 1-inch headspace.

4. Wipe the jar rims with a washcloth dipped in vinegar. Place the lid and ring on each jar and hand tighten.

5. Process in a pressure canner at 10 PSI or according to your elevation and canner type. Process quart jars for 90 minutes and pint jars for 75 minutes.

Teriyaki King Oyster Mushrooms

Enjoy this beautifully flavored dish inspired by Chinese cuisine. Depending on the size of the king oyster mushrooms, you may leave them whole or slice them in half. Toss these beauties with steamed broccoli and serve them over a bed of jasmine rice.

PREP TIME: **10 minutes**   **COOK TIME:** **25 minutes**
PROCESS TIME: **55 or 45 minutes**   **YIELD:** **5 quarts or 10 pints**

DIRECTIONS

1. Do not rinse or soak your mushrooms—simply wipe them clean with a damp paper towel one at a time. If the base of the mushroom is dirty, rinse the base to remove any dirt or debris, then pat it dry. Set aside.

2. Heat 2 tablespoons of the oil in a stockpot over medium-high heat. Working in batches, add 5 to 6 mushrooms and brown each side for 2 minutes, being careful not to overcrowd the stockpot. Remove the mushrooms and set them aside.

3. In the same stockpot, add any remaining oil and the onion, sugar, ginger, and garlic and cook for about 15 minutes or until the onion starts to caramelize. Slowly add the coconut aminos and sake and deglaze the pan. Add 4 cups of the water to the stockpot and bring it to a boil.

4. Whisk together the remaining 2 cups of water and the ClearJel and add it to the stockpot. Boil it for 1 minute, stirring constantly, then add the mushrooms back into the stockpot and stir to blend and coat the mushrooms. Remove from heat.

5. Using a funnel and a slotted spoon, ladle the mushrooms into each jar and pack the jars tight using the headspace-measuring tool, filling each jar to 1 inch of headspace. Next, ladle the sauce into each jar, leaving 1 inch of headspace. Remove any trapped air pockets and add additional sauce if necessary to maintain the 1-inch headspace.

6. Wipe the jar rims with a washcloth dipped in vinegar. Place the lid and ring on each jar and hand tighten.

7. Process in a pressure canner at 10 PSI or according to your elevation and canner type. Process quart jars for 55 minutes and pint jars for 45 minutes.

INGREDIENTS

4½ lbs. king oyster mushrooms (about 25 to 30)

1 cup peanut oil, divided

1 red onion, diced (1½ cup)

½ cup packed brown sugar

2 T. ginger paste

6 garlic cloves, minced (1 T.)

1 cup coconut aminos or soy sauce

1 cup sake

6 cups water, divided

½ cup ClearJel

INGREDIENT TIP: *While this recipe is intended for king oyster mushrooms, you truly may use any mushroom in its place. Some delicious suggestions are baby portobellas, porcini, or shiitake mushrooms. Be sure to weigh the mushrooms to ensure you keep the same jar yield.*

Vegetable Marsala

The rich and flavorful sauce incorporated with a variety of vegetables makes this vegetable marsala a game changer. The combination of mushrooms, eggplant, and squash creates a hearty dish with robust flavor and a touch of natural sweetness. Enjoy it over a bed of rice or buttered noodles.

PREP TIME: 30 minutes   COOK TIME: 30 minutes
PROCESS TIME: 75 or 55 minutes   YIELD: 8 quarts or 16 pints

DIRECTIONS

1. Place the butter in a stockpot and melt it over medium-high heat. Add the onion, garlic, and mushrooms and cook for about 15 to 20 minutes or until the onion is translucent and the mushrooms have reduced in size by almost half.

2. Slowly add the wine and broth, mixing well. Bring it to a boil, then stir in the squash, eggplant, tomatoes, parsley, rosemary, salt, red pepper flakes, and sugar. Return it to a boil, then reduce the heat and simmer for 10 minutes, being sure not to overcook it.

3. Using a funnel, ladle the mixture into jars, leaving a 1-inch headspace. Remove any trapped air pockets and add additional sauce if necessary to maintain the 1-inch headspace.

4. Wipe the jar rims with a washcloth dipped in vinegar. Place the lid and ring on each jar and hand tighten.

5. Process in a pressure canner at 10 PSI or according to your elevation and canner type. Process quart jars for 75 minutes and pint jars for 55 minutes.

INGREDIENTS

3 T. butter

1 large sweet onion, diced (2 cups)

1 head garlic, peeled and minced (¼ cup)

3½ lbs. white mushrooms, sliced (18 cups)

3 cups pinot noir

3 cups vegetable broth

2 acorn squash, peeled and cut into 1-inch cubes (7 cups)

1 eggplant, cut into 1-inch cubes (4½ cups)

9 Roma tomatoes, diced (3 cups)

½ bunch parsley, finely chopped (½ cup)

3 tsp. crushed dried rosemary

2 tsp. salt

1 to 3 tsp. red pepper flakes

1 tsp. sugar (optional)

Vegetable Pot Pie Filling

Pot pie filling is a popular meal to have in the pantry and can be used in so many ways. The obvious use is to bake a pie; however, you may also heat a jar and serve it over biscuits or thick egg noodles or use it when making casseroles. The sky is the limit with this home-canned recipe.

PREP TIME: 20 minutes **COOK TIME:** 15 minutes
PROCESS TIME: 75 or 60 minutes **YIELD:** 8 quarts or 16 pints

INGREDIENTS

4 T. butter

1 large sweet onion, diced (2 cups)

8 celery ribs, diced (2 cups)

8 carrots, peeled and diced (4 cups)

1 head garlic, peeled and minced (¼ cup)

5 cups green peas (fresh or frozen)

5 cups green beans (fresh or frozen), cut into 1-inch pieces

2 cups corn kernels (fresh or frozen)

1½ cups cauliflower florets (fresh or frozen)

1½ cups broccoli florets (fresh or frozen)

6 cups vegetable broth, divided

2 tsp. salt (optional)

1 tsp. black pepper

1 cup ClearJel

DIRECTIONS

1. Melt the butter in a large stockpot over medium-high heat. Add the onion, celery, carrots, and garlic and cook them for about 10 minutes or until the onion is translucent and the celery is soft. Add the peas, green beans, corn, cauliflower, broccoli, 4 cups of the broth, salt, and pepper and mix well. Bring it to a boil.

2. Whisk together the remaining 2 cups of broth with the ClearJel to create a slurry. Slowly add the slurry to the stockpot, stirring continuously. Reduce the heat to medium and gently boil the filling for an additional 5 minutes, stirring often, then remove from heat. (If the filling begins to get too thick while cooking, add water in ½ cup increments to achieve the desired consistency.)

3. Using a funnel, ladle the filling into jars, leaving a 1-inch headspace. Remove any trapped air pockets and add additional filling if necessary to maintain the 1-inch headspace.

4. Wipe the jar rims with a washcloth dipped in vinegar. Place the lid and ring on each jar and hand tighten.

5. Process in a pressure canner at 10 PSI or according to your elevation and canner type. Process quart jars for 75 minutes and pint jars for 60 minutes.

RECIPE TIP: *There are 23 cups of vegetables in this pie filling. If you prefer one over another, you may omit any vegetable and increase the quantity of another so long as your recipe yields the required 23 cups.*

Vegetable Stew

A pantry isn't complete without stew. Enjoy having this vegetarian delight available any time of the year. It is loaded with chopped veggies and portobella mushrooms, has a rich cabernet broth, and encompasses all the fun flavors rosemary and thyme have to offer. Bon appétit!

PREP TIME: 35 minutes   COOK TIME: 30 minutes
PROCESS TIME: 75 or 60 minutes   YIELD: 8 quarts or 16 pints

DIRECTIONS

1. Heat the oil in a stockpot over medium-high heat. Add the mushrooms, onion, celery, garlic, thyme, and rosemary and mix well. Cook until the onion is translucent and the mushrooms have reduced in size, about 20 minutes. Add the broth, water, wine, and tomato paste and stir until the paste has fully dispersed. Bring to a boil.

2. Add the remaining ingredients to the stockpot, mix well, and return to a boil. Reduce heat to medium and boil gently for 10 minutes. Remove bay leaves and discard.

3. Using a funnel, ladle the stew into jars, leaving a 1-inch headspace. Remove any trapped air pockets and add additional stew if necessary to maintain the 1-inch headspace.

4. Wipe the jar rims with a washcloth dipped in vinegar. Place the lid and ring on each jar and hand tighten.

5. Process in a pressure canner at 10 PSI or according to your elevation and canner type. Process quart jars for 75 minutes and pint jars for 60 minutes.

INGREDIENTS

3 T. olive oil

32 oz. portobella mushrooms, sliced (8 cups)

2 white onions, chopped (2½ cups)

4 celery ribs, chopped (1 cup)

1 head garlic, peeled and minced (¼ cup)

2 tsp. dried thyme

1 tsp. dried crushed rosemary

8 cups vegetable broth

3 cups water

1 cup red wine (cabernet)

1 (12 oz.) can tomato paste

4 carrots, peeled and chopped (4 cups)

6 red-skinned potatoes, cut into 1-inch cubes (4 cups)

¼ cup packed dark brown sugar

3 T. coconut aminos or soy sauce

3 bay leaves

2 tsp. ground coriander

1 tsp. black pepper

Index

ACKNOWLEDGMENTS

As I get closer to being an empty nester, I look back at the past decade and thank my children, Caleb and Audrey, for their unfailing love and support, their understanding of my lofty goals, and for their tender words of encouragement when I needed them most. *Meals in a Jar* took two years to create and test, and another year to write and shoot photography. The most fun for me has been watching their reactions when taste-testing a new recipe or concept. I am proud to say they can both swiftly articulate what's "missing." And I will cherish the laughs we've had when a recipe totally bombed. Oh yes, there is much I will never live down (haha).

This book couldn't go to print without me mentioning my sweet li'l Mumma, who is a living testament to God's divine love and precious mercy. She continues to navigate life with an infectious smile and a twinkle in her eye, never letting on that her frail body is riddled with cancer. She continues to amaze us…and entertain us. Many a night she has sat with me at my kitchen table, chopping vegetables while the two of us chat away, stopping every so often to belly laugh when we hear a favorite quip from the Golden Girls playing in the background. I tell you, she and I have solved many of the world's problems while in the kitchen filling mason jars. Her strength and continued faith in Jesus has influenced me my whole life.

While I may have already dedicated *Meals in a Jar* to my sister, Deborah, I would be remiss not to mention why I did so. These past three years have been the hardest on me—on everyone really. And there have been many times I would call her crying, sharing my frustrations navigating the literary world, or after I took a beating from online haters. Each time, Deb would pick me up off the proverbial floor and help me see what I couldn't. She reminded me to be brave and have faith. As we age, I hold so dear our precious memories growing up, and I thank God for giving me a sister. "Put on a little lipstick, everything will be fine."

My cousins Lisa and Scott, Amy and Eren, Terry and Phil, and Missy, Natalie, and Emily have been my closest friends throughout my life, and even more so these past three years. Our deep bond grows stronger as we grow older, as our children grow older, and as we watch our parents age. My cousins are my first best friends, and we will always have one another's backs.

I must acknowledge my prayer warrior Aunt Diane, who left us to be with the Lord. I was proud to be named after her and always got a chuckle when the whole family got together, when I would officially become "Diane Number 2" for the day. I will forever miss her wall-shaking prayers, her feisty attitude, her capacity to love, and her full-belly laugh. She "got me."

I would also like to acknowledge my friend Carrie, who has helped me gain knowledge and perspective on the vegetarian lifestyle. It was her inspiration that led me to create and expand canning recipes for those who prefer not to eat meat. She leads me to dig deeper into meatless meals and meat alternatives, working hard to create and test new canning recipes so I may reach more home canners. Our time together with her friends and family in Tennessee is something I will always cherish and for which I will forever be grateful. I see her as a kindred spirit working diligently to live off God's land with care and responsibility for our fellow man.

I am so thankful for my friend and fellow author Terri DeBoer. It was her gracious introduction to my amazingly talented agent, Tom Dean, that put this project's wheels in motion. I am so grateful to Tom for taking a chance on his first cookbook author and helping me take my ideas to the next level. You have been a joy to work with and I look forward to a long and prosperous partnership. Through Tom I met my editor, Heather Green. She and I formed an instant connection, and I just knew she, too, was a kindred spirit. I believe God purposely placed these three amazing people in my life for so much more than the printed page, but to be His vessels.

And to my friend (and amazing food photographer) Jeff Hage and his amazing parents, Elaine and Marcel: We may not be blood, but we are family. I am so blessed to know the Hage family and to be loved and supported over the years. I will forever hold dear the many memories of prepping food, canning, cooking, and breaking bread together.

God has blessed me immensely and I owe everything to Him.

About the Author

Diane Devereaux, The Canning Diva®, is a nationally syndicated food preservation expert, author, television presenter, instructor, and mother of two. Since 2012, Devereaux has been sharing her lifetime passion of canning and food preservation, translating it to the busy lives of families across the globe. She is a life-long resident of Michigan and fellow canner who has been home canning and preserving food for over 30 years.

Diane Devereaux received her bachelor's in international business from Davenport University and later plunged into a career in disaster management, where she applied her skills in food preservation, survival, and sustainability to those in crisis. Her background in home canning combined with her tenure in disaster management led Diane to create The Canning Diva®, where she blended her passion for gardening and preserving with her knowledge of preparedness and self-reliance.

Diane is a huge advocate for individuals having the right to know the contents of what they ingest and is a proud supporter of honest and forthright labeling of all foods. It is because of this belief she chooses home canning throughout the year to ensure a healthy lifestyle for herself and her family. She has made it her goal to teach the time-honored traditions of canning and food preservation across every corner of the world, which is the driving force of all she creates, writes, and speaks.

WWW.CANNINGDIVA.COM